Time for Portuguese

All it takes is twenty minutes a day

Sue Tyson-Ward

Stanley Thornes (Publishers) Ltd

First published in 1999 by:
Stanley Thornes (Publishers) Ltd
Ellenborough House
Wellington Street
CHELTENHAM GL50 1YW
England

A catalogue record for this book is available
from the British Library

99 00 01 02 03 / 10 9 8 7 6 5 4 3 2 1

ISBN 0-7487-3884-3 (book)
ISBN 0-7487-3886-X (complete pack)
ISBN 0-7487-3885-1 (cassettes)

Also available in the *Time for Languages* series:

Time for French, Paul Durrant
Time for German, Corinna Schicker
Time for Italian, Donatella de Ferra, Marina Mozzon-McPherson
Time for Spanish, Robert Clarke

Cover: Joanna Kerr

Typeset by Action Publishing Technology Limited, Gloucester
Recorded at the Speech Recording Studio, London
Voice artists: Edite Phillips, João Duarte Ferreira, Carlos Alves
Printed and bound in Great Britain by T. J. International Ltd, Padstow, Cornwall

How to make the best use of *Time for Portuguese*

The material in *Time for Portuguese* has been designed for you to complete one unit every day, but you are in control. If you want to cover several units in a day, then do that. Do try, however, to stick to a sensible routine so that you cover a number of units spread over the course of one week, rather than ten sessions at the weekend. You will retain so much more if you 'drip-feed' yourself. You should ideally work through the units in sequence, but again, you are in control. Choose a method which suits you best.

Start by reading the **Vocabulário** (vocabulary) section. Then listen to the **Diálogo** (dialogue) section, first of all without following the transcript in the book, and then using the text. This uses the words you have been practising already. See how much you can understand before you consult the text. Don't worry if there are parts you miss – just try to catch the drift of what is said.

Once you have read through the text and unravelled its contents you are ready for the exercises (**Actividades**). Some of these involve the recording, some don't. In Exercise 3 of every unit you will be asked to take part in a speaking activity. Usually this takes the form of a dialogue with an actor on the recording. You will be given prompts in English on the recording. These are either written in the book or shown by means of pictures. Make sure you follow the sequence of these prompts carefully to guide you in your responses. You will soon get used to the method used here, and you will find it invaluable in gaining confidence in speaking naturally.

Finally read the **Língua** (usually a grammar hint) and **De interesse**, which gives you some background on the culture and lifestyle of Portuguese-speaking Europe.

Do come back to units in the future to refresh your memory. Once you have covered the unit with the help of the book, you will find that playing the recordings in your car or wherever will prove invaluable.

Good luck and enjoy learning Portuguese!

Contents

People

Introductions

Vocabulário (Vocabulary)

bom dia	hello, good morning
bem-vinda (a)	welcome (to)
muito bem	very well, well then
muito prazer	very pleased to meet you
obrigada	thank you
igualmente	likewise
como se chama?	what's your name?
chamo-me ...	my name is ...
de onde é?	where are you from?
sou (de)	I am (from)
sou inglês	I am an English man
sou inglesa	I am an English woman
a Inglaterra	England
no norte	to/in the north

Diálogo (Dialogue)

Anne	Bom dia. Sou Anne Green. Como se chama o senhor?
António	Chamo-me António da Silva.
Anne	Muito prazer.
António	Igualmente. De onde é, Anne?
Anne	Sou inglesa. Sou de Manchester, no norte da Inglaterra.
António	Muito bem. Bem-vinda a Portugal, Anne.
Anne	Obrigada.

Actividades (Exercises)

1 Fill in the following speech bubbles as if you are the person, giving your name and the town you come from. The first one is an example for you.
(*Answers on page 126.*)

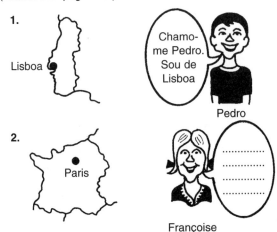

1.

Lisboa

Chamo-me Pedro. Sou de Lisboa

Pedro

2.

Paris

Françoise

3.

Londres

Mark

4.

Berlim

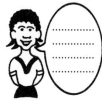

Helga

2 Listen to the recording of three people saying who they are and where they are from in Portugal. Fill in their details on the table below. (*Answers on page 126.*)

	Name	From
1.		
2.		
3.		

3 Now take part in a dialogue using the English prompts below to guide you. (*Answers on the recording and on page 126.*)

1. Good morning, my name is Frank.
2. I am English, I am from Lancaster.
3. I am pleased to meet you too.

Língua (Language)

You do not necessarily need to use the word for 'I' (**eu**), as the verb forms demonstrate who is speaking: **Sou**, '(I) am'; **chamo**, '(I) am called'.
Adjectives (words of description, such as for nationality) have different forms for male and female. Usually the male form ends in **-o**, and the female in **-a**.

| **americano** American man | **americana** American woman |

There are exceptions to spelling, and you will see there is no **-o** on the male form here:

| **inglês** English (man) | **inglesa** English (woman) |

These changes apply to other words:

| **bem-vindo** welcome (to male) | **bem-vinda** welcome (to female) |
| **obrigado** thank you (said by male) | **obrigada** thank you (said by female) |

De interesse (Of interest)

There are many ways of saying 'you' in Portuguese, depending on how formal you are being. The Portuguese people in general show respect when talking to strangers, older people, or those in a superior (work or social) position. For most of your dealings you will hear/use **o senhor/a senhora** (literally, 'the gentleman'/ 'the lady'), or simply the verb without the word for 'you', as in the dialogue: **De onde é?** (literally, 'From where are [you]?').

Eating out

Snacks and drinks

Vocabulário

boa tarde	hello, good afternoon
faz favor!	please/excuse me!
se faz favor	please, if you please
diga	can I help you? (lit. 'say')
queria ...	I would like ...
mais alguma coisa?	anything else?
sim	yes
não	no
uma empada de galinha	a small chicken pie
um pastel de nata	a custard cake
um café	a small black coffee
uma água mineral	a mineral water
sem gás	still (not fizzy)
com gás	fizzy
fresca	chilled
natural	at room temperature
ou	or
e	and

Diálogo

customer	Faz favor!
waiter	Boa tarde. Diga, se faz favor.
customer	Queria um café e uma água mineral sem gás.
waiter	Fresca ou natural?
customer	Fresca, se faz favor.
waiter	Mais alguma coisa?
customer	Sim, um pastel de nata e uma empada de galinha. Obrigada.
waiter	Obrigado.

Actividades

1   Fill in the gaps in these sentences, according to the pictures.
    (*Answers on page 126.*)

1.   Queria ...., se faz favor.

2.   Queria ...., se faz favor.

3.   Queria .... e ...., se faz favor.

2   Listen to the recording of two people ordering snacks and drinks from a café. Tick the boxes with details of what they order on the table below. (*Answers on page 126.*)

	um café	uma água mineral	um pastel de nata	uma empada
1.				
2.				

3   Now take part in a dialogue using the English prompts to guide you. (*Answers on the recording and on page 126.*)

1. I would like a chicken pie.
2. Yes, I would like a mineral water, please.
3. Chilled.
4. Fizzy.

Língua

All nouns (objects) in Portuguese are divided into masculine and feminine words. Usually, words ending in **-o** are masculine, and those in **-a** are feminine.

masculine	*feminine*
um garoto (a small white coffee)	**uma água** (a water)

There are also many exceptions to this rule, so be prepared to learn them as you go along.

um café   (a black coffee)
um pastel   (a cake, pastry)

The masculine and feminine words for 'a/an/one' are **um** and **uma** respectively.

De interesse

There is a great variety of coffees in Portugal – catering for every imaginable need. You could ask for: **um café** (**uma bica** in Lisbon), for a small, espresso-style, black coffee; **um garoto**, for a small white coffee; or **um galão**, for a milky coffee served in a glass. There is also **um pingado** – a small, black coffee with a drop of milk; **uma italiana** – a very strong espresso; **um café com leite** – white coffee in a normal sized cup.

Accomodation

Booking a room in a hotel

Diálogo

customer	Boa noite. Têm quartos vagos?
receptionist	Boa noite, senhora. Sim, temos. Para quantas pessoas?
customer	Para três.
receptionist	Querem quartos individuais?
customer	Não. Queríamos um quarto de casal e um individual.
receptionist	É para quantas noites?
customer	Para cinco.
receptionist	Está bem. Temos os quartos nove e seis.

Actividades

1   Match the guests to their rooms by drawing a line to the appropriate picture.
(*Answers on page 126.*)

1. Queria um quarto individual.   **a)**

2. Queriamos um quarto de casal.   **b)**

3. Queriamos dois quartos individuais.   **c)**

2 Listen to the recording of two people asking for hotel rooms and fill in the table below, according to their requirements. (*Answers on page 126.*)

	number of people	number of nights	single room(s)	double room(s)
1.				
2.				

3 Now take part in a dialogue using the English prompts on the cassette and in your book to guide you. (*Answers on the recording and on page 126.*)

    1. Good morning, do you have any rooms free?
    2. For one.
    3. For five.

Língua

The numbers 'one' and 'two' have two forms: masculine and feminine.

masculine	*feminine*
um one	**uma** one
dois two	**duas** two

Your choice of form depends on whether the object following the number is masculine or feminine, thus:

um quarto one/a room	**uma noite** one/a night
dois quartos two rooms	**duas pessoas** two people

You will also find in the dialogue some plural forms of words. Usually the plural (ie. when there is more than one) is formed by simply adding an **-s** to a word, although there are exceptions.

singular	*plural*
um quarto one room	**cinco quartos** five rooms
um quarto individual one single	**três quartos individuais** three singles

De interesse

There are, in fact, several ways of specifying your hotel room. 'A single room', as in our dialogue, is **um quarto individual**, or **um quarto simples**. 'A double room' can be **um quarto de casal** or **um quarto duplo**. Usually, a double room will have two single beds in it (**com duas camas**). If you specifically want a double bed, you may have to request a room **com cama de casal**.

UNIT 4

Travel

A bus journey

Vocabulário

desculpe	excuse me
éste é ...?	is this/this is ...?
não, não é	no, it's not
é, sim	yes, it is
o autocarro	the bus
um bilhete	a ticket
bilhetes	tickets
de ida	single
de ida e volta	return
quanto tempo leva?	how long does it take?
só	only
minutos	minutes
onze	11
doze	12
treze	13
catorze	14
quinze	15
dezasseis	16
dezassete	17
dezoito	18
dezanove	19
vinte	20

Diálogo

woman	Este é o autocarro para Faro?
bus driver 1	Não, não é.
woman	Desculpe, este é o autocarro para Faro?
bus driver 2	É, sim.
woman	Queria dois bilhetes, se faz favor.
bus driver 2	De ida, ou de ida e volta?
woman	De ida e volta. Quanto tempo leva?
bus driver 2	Só quinze minutos.
woman	Obrigada.

Actividades

1 Respond to the questions below as if you were the driver of each bus, writing your answer in the space provided. We have answered the first for you.
(*Answers on page 126.*)

1.    Este é o autocarro para Lisboa?   *É sim.*

2. Este é o autocarro para Faro? ....

3. Este é o autocarro para Braga? ....

4. Este é o autocarro para Silves? ....

2 Listen to three people on the tape, asking for tickets to different destinations, then decide whether the following statements are true (**verdadeiro**) or false (**falso**). (*Answers on page 126.*)

	wants	to	V	F
1.	return ticket	Carvoeiro		
2.	2 single tickets	Évora		
3.	2 returns	Fátima		

3 Three people will ask you about journey times. Use the information below and tell them how long each trip takes. (*Answers on the recording and on page 126.*)

1. To Lisboa: 17 minutes
2. To Faro: 13 minutes
3. To Estoril: 19 minutes

Língua

You can work out a pattern to help you learn the numbers in Portuguese. Look at numbers 11–15; they all have the same ending (**-ze**), and the English word 'dozen' may help you to remember the number 12. Numbers 16–19 are based on 10 plus the last digit, thus 17 = **dez as sete**. Listen to the tape a few times to practise the pronunciation, then try saying all the numbers backwards from 20.

There are four variations for the article 'the' in Portuguese:

	singular	*plural*
masculine	**o autocarro**	**os bilhetes**
feminine	**a pessoa**	**as noites**

De interesse

If you are travelling by bus within a city or its close boundaries, you can buy a book of pre-paid tickets, often called **módulos**, which are cheaper than individual tickets. As you enter the bus, you 'click' the ticket in a small clipper machine.

 **Directions**

Getting to the tourist office

Vocabulário

há	there is/are; is/are there?
um posto de turismo	a tourist office
aqui	here
fica	it is (situated)
longe	far
perto	near
na praça	in the square
da praça	of the square
vira	(you) turn
segue em frente	(you) carry straight on
à esquerda, do lado esquerdo	left, on/to the left (-hand side)
à direita, do lado direito	right, on/to the right (-hand side)
pode repetir?	can you repeat?
mais devagar	more slowly
claro	of course
de nada	don't mention it
a pé	on foot

Diálogo

visitor	Desculpe, há um posto de turismo aqui?
woman	Sim, há um na Praça de São Jorge.
visitor	Fica muito longe?
woman	Não, fica perto. O senhor vira aqui à esquerda, segue em frente, e o turismo fica do lado direito da praça.
visitor	Desculpe, pode repetir mais devagar, se faz favor?
woman	Claro. O senhor vira aqui à esquerda, segue em frente, e o turismo fica do lado direito da praça. Leva só dez minutos a pé.
visitor	Muito obrigado.
woman	De nada.

à esquerda   em frente   à direita

Actividades

1   Indicate whether the directions with each map will lead you to the tourist office, underlining **sim** (yes) or **não** (no). (*Answers on page 126.*)

1.

O senhor segue em frente, vira à esquerda, vira à direita, e o turismo fica em frente.

sim   ou   **não**

2.

O senhor segue em frente, vira à esquerda, e o turismo fica à direita.

sim ou **não**

2 Listen to someone on the tape receiving directions to the tourist office and note down, in English, the information they are given on the table below. Listen to the whole exercise before taking notes. (*Answers on page 126.*)

First	then	next (2 instructions)	then	where is the office?

3 Now take part in a dialogue yourself, using the English prompts to help you and speaking in the pauses on the recording. (*Answers on the recording and on page 126.*)

1. Excuse me, is there a tourist office here?
2. Is it very far?
3. Can you repeat it a bit slower, please?
4. Thank you.

Língua

In the dialogue you came across the expressions *na* **praça** (in the square), and *da* **praça** (of the square). These forms have come from a combination of words, contracted (ie. squashed together) to ease pronunciation.

	+ o	+ a	+ os	+ as	the
em in/on	**no**	**na**	**nos**	**nas**	in/on the
de of/from	**do**	**da**	**dos**	**das**	of/from the

You will find other contracted words as you work through the course.

De interesse

Most Portuguese people do speak rather quickly, and you may experience some trouble understanding their initial responses to your questions. It is particularly awkward in the Algarve, where they tend to 'chop off' the beginnings and endings of words; thus the word **escudo** (the Portuguese unit of currency), may sound like 'scud'.

Town amenities

At the tourist office

Vocabulário

(as) informações	(the) information	(a) segunda(-feira)	Monday
(as) excursões	(the) trips, excursions	(a) terça(-feira)	Tuesday
a excursão	the trip	(a) quarta(-feira)	Wednesday
um folheto	a leaflet	(a) quinta(-feira)	Thursday
uma lista	a list	(a) sexta(-feira)	Friday
a cidade	the city, town	(o) sábado	Saturday
o hotel	the hotel	(o) domingo	Sunday
(os) hotéis	(the) hotels		
(as) reservas	(the) reservations		
fazer	to make, do		
visitar	to visit		
posso ...?	may/can I ...?		
pode	you can		
aqui tem	here you have		
aqui está	here you are, here is ...		
com certeza	certainly		
sobre	about, on		
onde	where		
quando	when		
lá	there		
às terças	on Tuesdays		
às quintas	on Thursdays		

Diálogo

visitor	Boa tarde. Têm informações sobre Lisboa?
tourism agent	Temos, sim. Aqui tem um folheto sobre a cidade e uma lista de hotéis.
visitor	Posso fazer reservas para excursões aqui?
agent	Pode, sim. Para onde?
visitor	Queria visitar Évora. Quando há excursões para lá?
agent	Há excursões às terças e às quintas.
visitor	Bom, queria um bilhete para quinta-feira, se faz favor.
agent	Com certeza. Aqui está.

Actividades

1 Match the English statements to what people are saying in Portuguese. (*Answers on page 126.*)

1. Sylvia wants a list of hotels and a trip to Faro for Saturday.

a) Queria um folheto sobre o Porto, um bilhete para Faro para a quarta-feira, e um bilhete para a Nazaré para a segunda-feira.

2. John wants a leaflet about Évora, a trip to Nazaré on Sunday and a list of hotels.

b)
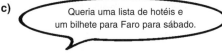
Queria um bilhete para a Nazaré para domingo, uma lista de hotéis e um folheto sobre Évora.

c)
Queria uma lista de hotéis e um bilhete para Faro para sábado.

3. Frank wants a trip to Faro for Wednesday, a leaflet on Oporto, and an excursion to Nazaré on Monday.

d)
Queria um bilhete para Faro para quinta-feira e uma lista de hotéis.

2 Listen to two people on the tape booking excursions at a tourist office, and fill in the table below according to the reservations they make. (*Answers on page 126.*)

	excursion to?	which day?
1.		
2.		

3 Now try re-creating the dialogue from the opposite page, using the prompts on the recording to guide you. (*Answers on the recording and on page 126.*)

1. Good morning.
2. Do you have information on Oporto?
3. Can I book excursions here?
4. To Fátima.
5. I would like two tickets for Wednesday.

Língua

There are a few examples in the dialogue of words in the plural which do not belong to the simple **+s** formation as in Unit 3.

ending	singular		plural	
+ão	**a excursão**	trip	**as excursões**	trips
	a informação	information	**as informações**	information
+l	**o hotel**	hotel	**os hotéis**	hotels

Unfortunately, there are many exceptions to the rules, so learn irregular words as you go along.

De interesse

The days of the week (**os dias da semana**) in Portuguese are mostly unlike those in the other Latin-based languages, apart from the two days of the weekend. As Monday in fact starts as the second (**segunda**) day, followed by the third (**terça**), you can count through up to Saturday. In practice the **-feira** part of the expression is dropped in spoken Portuguese.

UNIT 7 The town centre

Where can I ...?

Vocabulário

onde é que ...?	where (is it that) ...?
comprar	to buy
mandar consertar	to have mended, to mend
o pão	the bread
a padaria	the bakery
o(s) sapato(s)	the shoe(s)
o sapateiro	the shoe mender
o livro	the book
a livraria	the bookshop
a mercearia	the grocer's
a farmácia	the chemist's
o banco	the bank
o talho	the butcher's
a carne	meat
outra coisa	another thing
na esquina	on the corner
ao pé de	right next to
pois	well, er ...
bem	well, well then
obrigadinha	thanks very much

Diálogo

woman	Desculpe, onde é que posso comprar pão?
man	Pão? Pois, há uma padaria na esquina.
woman	Obrigada. Ah, outra coisa, onde é que posso mandar consertar os sapatos?
man	Os sapatos? Bem, há um sapateiro na praça, ao pé do banco.
woman	Obrigadinha.
man	De nada. Bom dia.

Actividades

1 Draw a line from the pictures to place the items in the correct shops.
(*Answers on page 126.*)

1.   2.   3.   4.   5.

a) o talho   b) a livraria   c) a farmácia   d) o sapateiro   e) a padaria

2 Listen to two people asking where they can buy various items, and write down where they are sent. (*Answers on page 126.*)

1. ....

2. ....

3 Now it's your turn to take part in a dialogue. Follow the prompts and speak in the pauses. (*Answers on the recording and on page 126.*)

1. Excuse me, where can I buy a book?
2. Thank you. Ah, another thing – where can I buy some meat?
3. Thanks very much.

Língua

In Unit 3 you learned that the numeral 'one' (**um**, **uma**) was also the word for 'a/an', and that it had both a masculine and feminine form. We can see it being used in the dialogue opposite, in **uma padaria** (a baker's), **um sapateiro** (a shoe mender's). The plural forms of these words, which correspond to the English 'some' are **uns** (m. pl.) and **umas** (f. pl.), thus:

uns jornais   (some newspapers)   **umas laranjas**   (some oranges)

In practice, however, you will find that the Portuguese do not use a word for 'some' in most conversational situations:

Queria comprar jornais.   I would like to buy (some) newspapers.

De interesse

The word **pois** is the Portuguese equivalent of saying 'er' or 'well'. It is extremely common, and is a useful prop if you can't immediately find your next word.

The form of **obrigado** which is in the dialogue – **obrigadinha** – is known as a diminutive (or smaller) form. Again, this is very common, as it is considered more friendly. Remember, if you are a man you would say **obrigadinho**. Listen out for these **-inho/-inha** forms when you are in Portugal.

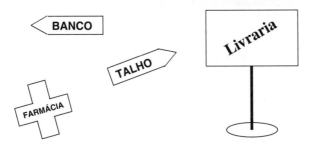

Personal choices

Likes and dislikes

Vocabulário

olá	hi, hello there
então	(well) then
também	also
mas	but
porque	because
gosta (de)?	do you like?
eu	I
gosto	I (do) like
acho (que)	I think (that)
prefiro	I prefer
ver	to see
pessoalmente	personally
muito (muitos)	a lot, much (many)
não muito	not much
menos	less
mais	more
cara	expensive
(o) trânsito	traffic
(o) comércio	business
(a) igreja	church

Diálogo

woman	Olá, João, bom dia. Então, gosta de Lisboa?
man	Gosto, sim. Há muito para fazer.
woman	Eu também gosto, mas acho que prefiro Coimbra – há menos trânsito. O João gosta de Coimbra?
man	Gosto, mas não muito. Pessoalmente, prefiro o Porto porque há mais comércio.
woman	E Braga? Gosta?
man	Gosto muito. Há muitas igrejas para ver.

Actividades

1 Look at what the following people are saying about various places, and decide which of the cities they would prefer to be in. (*Answers on page 126.*)

1.
Gosto de Londres e Paris, mas prefiro Madrid.

a) Lisboa

2.
Gosto muito de Lisboa. Não gosto de Madrid – é muito cara.

b) Paris

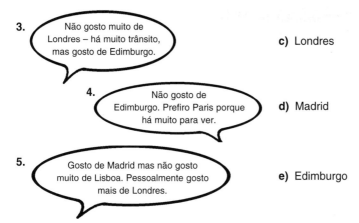

3. Não gosto muito de Londres – há muito trânsito, mas gosto de Edimburgo.

c) Londres

4. Não gosto de Edimburgo. Prefiro Paris porque há muito para ver.

d) Madrid

5. Gosto de Madrid mas não gosto muito de Lisboa. Pessoalmente gosto mais de Londres.

e) Edimburgo

2 Listen to José and Ana talking about which cities they like and dislike, and mark their responses on the table. (*Answers on page 126.*)

	José		Ana	
	gosta	não gosta	gosta	não gosta
Braga				
Lisboa				
Albufeira				
Porto				

3 Now take part in an interview about your likes and dislikes of various cities. Follow the prompts on the tape to guide you. (*Answers on the recording and on page 126.*)

1. I like it very much, there is a lot to see.
2. No. I don't like Paris very much.
3. Yes, I prefer Madrid because there is a lot to do.

Língua

In the dialogue we found the word **muito** used for three very different meanings:

1. 'a lot of things':   **Há *muito* para fazer.**   There is a lot to do.
2. 'much':   **Gosto *muito*.**   I like much/a lot.
3. 'many':   **Há *muitas igrejas*.**   There are many churches.

Note that when muito means 'much' or 'many' when used with a noun, its ending will change according to the noun that follows it:

muito*s* livr*os*   **muit*a* água**   **muit*o* temp*o*.**

De interesse

There is a Portuguese saying about the main cities in Portugal:
Coimbra canta, Braga reza, Lisboa desfila e o Porto trabalha, which means 'Coimbra sings, Braga prays, Lisbon parades and Oporto works', referring to distinct characteristics of those cities.

UNIT 9 Holidays

Discussing your holiday

Vocabulário

está	you are (polite)
estou	I am
é	is
estão	are
adoro	I love
pretendo	I intend
passar	to spend (time)
boas férias	(have a) good holiday
de férias	on holiday
de negócios	on business
(de) primavera	(of) spring
(o) castelo	castle
as amendoeiras	the almond trees
a Capela dos Ossos	the Chapel of Bones (see **De Interesse**)
bonito	pretty
faz calor	it is hot
tanto	so (much), too
é verdade	that's true
outra vez	again
agora	now
cá	here

Diálogo

man	Olá, Joana. Está cá outra vez?
Joana	Estou, sim. Gosto muito de Portugal.
man	Mas, está aqui de férias ou de negócios?
Joana	De férias. Adoro passar as férias de primavera em Portugal, porque é muito bonito e não faz tanto calor.
man	É verdade – no Algarve as amendoeiras estão muito bonitas agora.
Joana	Pretendo visitar Évora e ver a Capela dos Ossos.
man	Então, boas férias!

Actividades

1   Fill in the gaps in this exercise with either **é** (is) or **são** (are), and make the adjective agree with the object(s) in the pictures. Follow the example. (*Answers on page 126.*)

 1.   A Luisa é bonit*a*.

bonito

3.   Os sapatos .... bonit ......

bonito

 2.   O hotel ..... pequen .....

pequeno (small)

4.   As laranjas .... barat ....

barato (cheap)

5. A camisa ...... car ......

caro

2 Listen to Joana and Mr Oliveira talking about their holidays, and try to fill in the gaps in the dialogue below. (*Answers on page 126.*)

Joana	.... Sr Oliveira. Está .... de .... ou de ....?
Sr Oliveira	De .... Adoro passar .... em Portugal porque .... bonito e .... é muito ....
Joana	Sim, agora as cidades .... muito ....
Sr Oliveira	Pois, pretendo .... Lisboa e .... o Castelo de São Jorge.
Joana	............, boas fériás!

3 Now join in a dialogue based on the one on the opposite page. You will be prompted in English on the cassette. If you feel like stretching yourself, you can give your own reasons for liking places. (*Answers on the recording and on page 126.*)

1. Yes, I am. I like Portugal very much.
2. I'm on holiday, because it's not too hot and it's very pretty.
3. I intend to visit Évora.

Língua

By now, you have come across two different ways of saying 'you are' (**é/está**) and 'I am' (**sou/estou**). This is because Portuguese has two verbs 'to be': **ser** and **estar**. **Ser** is used mainly for permanent things and characteristics, people's origins, their nationality and profession. **Estar** is used mostly for temporary positions, locations and states. Here is the present tense of the two verbs in full:

	I am	*you are* (familiar)	*he/she/it is* *you are* (polite)	*we are*	*they are* *you are* (pl.)
ser	**sou**	**és**	**é**	**somos**	**são**
estar	**estou**	**estás**	**está**	**estamos**	**estão**

Sou inglês. I am English. (permanent characteristic/nationality)
Estou aqui de férias. I am here on holiday. (temporary situation)

Note also that there is both a polite and a familiar way of addressing someone as 'you': **o senhor/a senhora** and **tu** respectively.

De interesse

A Capela dos Ossos is a chapel with walls completely covered with bones and skulls. In fact, there are two such macabre buildings in Portugal: one in Évora and another in Faro. If you intend to enter them or any other religious building in Portugal, remember to wear appropriate clothing.

The weather

Talking about good weather

Vocabulário

(os) gelados	ice-creams
(os) sorvetes	ice-lollies
de laranja	(of) orange
de morango	(of) strawberry
que!	what/a !
ainda bem!	thank goodness
não é?	haven't we/isn't it? etc.
o tempo	the weather
o vento	the wind
o céu	the sky
as nuvens	the clouds
a nuvem	the cloud
azul	blue
hoje	today
tenho	I have

Diálogo

ice-cream vendor	Gelados! Gelados!
woman	Ainda bem! Três gelados, se faz favor.
ice-cream vendor	Tenho gelados de morango, e sorvetes de laranja e de morango.
woman	Bom, então dois sorvetes de laranja e um gelado.
ice-cream vendor	Muito bem. Que bom tempo temos, não é?
woman	Sim, faz muito calor e não há vento.
ice-cream vendor	O céu está azul e não há nuvens – está um dia bonito hoje.

Actividades

1 Match the pictures with the weather descriptions. (*Answers on page 126.*)

1.

a) Faz bom tempo.

2.

b) Não há nuvens.

3.

c) Faz muito calor.

4.

d) Há vento.

5.

e) Há nuvens.

2 Listen to the following weather forecast for three Portuguese cities, and mark the appropriate boxes in the table with a tick or a cross, according to what you hear. (*Answers on page 126.*)

	bom tempo	muito calor	céu azul	vento	nuvens
Guarda					
Lisboa					
Setúbal					

3 Now take part in a dialogue based on the one on the opposite page. Follow the English prompts and speak in the pauses on the recording. (*Answers on the recording and on page 126.*)

1. Thank goodness! I'd like five ice-creams, please.
2. Three strawberry ice-lollies and two ice-creams.
3. Yes, the sky is blue and there is no wind.

Língua

To talk about the weather, Portuguese uses a few different verbs, as you saw in the dialogue. Note the following:

fazer	**Faz calor**.	**Faz bom tempo**.
(to do, make)	It is hot.	It is good weather.
haver	**Há vento**.	**Há nuvens**.
(there is/are)	It is windy.	It is cloudy.
ter	**Temos bom tempo**.	
(to have)	We have nice weather.	
estar	**O céu está azul**.	
(to be)	The sky is blue.	
	O céu está nublado.	
	It is cloudy.	

Não é? If you know some French, you will notice that this expression is used like the French **n'est-ce pas?**, meaning 'isn't it?'

De interesse

In Portugal ice-cream vendors walk along beaches in the summer, with boxes full of ices. You can also buy snacks, such as crisps and nuts, from beach vendors.

III health

Precautions in the sun

Vocabulário

este	this (one) (masc.)
esta	this (one) (fem.)
bom/boa/bons/boas	good
solar	sun (adjective)
(o) sol	sun
queimaduras	burns
(o) creme	cream
(o) óleo	oil
bronzeador	tanning
(o) factor	factor
(a) pele	skin
(a) vez	time
vezes	times
claro/a	fair-(skin or hair colouring)
precisa (de)	you need
usar	to use
recomendo	I recommend
tomar cuidado	to take care

Diálogo

woman	Têm creme para queimaduras do sol?
pharmacist	Temos, sim, senhora. Este é muito bom. Precisa de usar duas vezes por dia.
woman	Obrigada. Também têm óleo bronzeador?
pharmacist	Temos, mas a pele da senhora é muito clara – precisa de usar um bom creme solar. Recomendo o factor número quinze. Este é bom.
woman	Obrigadinha. O sol está muito bom agora.
pharmacist	Claro que está, mas precisa de ter muito cuidado com o sol aqui em Portugal.

Actividades

1 To say 'this', you use **este** (masc.) or **esta** (fem.); to say 'these', you use **estes** (masc. pl.) or **estas** (fem. pl.). Decide which one is correct in each of the following sentences and then translate them into English. The first one is done to guide you. (*Answers on page 126.*)

1. *Esta* camisa é cara.   *This shirt is expensive.*

2. .... céu está azul.   ....

3. .... sapatos são bonitos.   ....

4. .... senhor é bonito.   ....

5. .... senhora é clara.   ....

6. .... sapatos não são caros.   ....

2 Listen to a pharmacist recommending sun creams of various factors to different people, and telling them how many times a day they must use them. Fill in the table below with your answers. (*Answers on page 126.*)

	factor no.	times per day
1.		
2.		

3 Now imagine you are the pharmacist and, for each person on the recording who asks you for sun cream, follow the instructions below for your recommendations. The presenter will guide you. (*Answers on the recording and on page 126.*)

	recommended factor	times per day
1.	15	3
2.	12	1

Língua

You will have noticed the words for 'good' in the **Vocabulário**. There are four forms:

	singular		plural	
masculine	**bom dia**	good morning	**bons sapatos**	good shoes
feminine	**boa noite**	good evening	**boas pessoas**	good people

The verb 'to need' in Portuguese is **precisar (de)**.

Precisa do creme.	You need the cream.
Precisa de usar um creme.	You need to use a cream.

De interesse

The sun in Portugal can be extremely hot in the summer months. TV warnings now advise people not to go to the beach between 3.00 and 6.00 p.m. Although the Portuguese do not take a real **siesta**, as their Spanish counterparts do, most shops close from 1.00 to 3.00 p.m., and sensible people sit inside in the cool.

Time

The best time for doing things

Vocabulário

ir	to go	vinte	20
à praia	to the beach	vinte e um/uma	21
da manhã (time)	in the morning	vinte e dois/duas	22
da tarde (time)	in the afternoon	vinte e três	23
(o) meio-dia	midday	vinte e quatro	24
depois (de)	after	vinte e cinco	25
as nove (horas)	nine o'clock	vinte e seis	26
as seis (horas)	six o'clock	vinte e sete	27
deveria	I/you/he/she/it should	vinte e oito	28
poderia	I/you/he/she/it could	vinte e nove	29
ficar	to stay	trinta	30
tome	take	quarenta	40
essa	that	cinquenta	50
aconselhável	advisable	sessenta	60
primeiro	first	setenta	70
melhor	better	oitenta	80
até	until	noventa	90
entre	between	cem/cento	100
com	with		
(o) cinema	cinema		

Diálogo

tourist	Qual é a melhor hora para ir à praia?
woman	Bom, agora, entre as nove da manhã e o meio-dia, ou depois das seis da tarde.
tourist	E quanto tempo deveria ficar?
woman	Pois, com essa pele clara, é aconselhável só ficar vinte e cinco minutos no primeiro dia.
tourist	E depois?
woman	Depois poderia ficar mais, até quarenta ou cinquenta minutos por dia, mas tome muito cuidado.

Actividades

1 Four people have asked how long they should stay on the beach. Match up the replies to the times indicated on the clocks. (*Answers on page 126.*)

1. Poderia ficar trinta e cinco minutos. **a)**

2. E aconselhável só ficar vinte minutos. **b)**

3. É melhor ficar quarenta minutos. **c)**

4. Poderia ficar cinquenta e cinco minutos. **d)**

2 Now listen to some numbers on the recording and circle those you hear. (*Answers on page 126.*)

55	96	31	78	24	49
62	34	29	83	97	57
43	71	38	66	45	92

3 The table below indicates how long you can stay safely on beaches around the world. Answer the questions on the tape by referring to the table. (*Answers on the recording and on page 126.*)

beach	number of minutes
Lisboa	48
Rio	22
California	34
Brighton	97
Alicante	55
Madeira	61

Língua

From the list opposite, you will be able to work out how numbers above 20 are put together. You simply insert the word **e** (and) between the two digits. You will notice this pattern occurring again when you move on to higher numbers.

If your last digit is a 1 or a 2, you always have to choose between the masculine or feminine forms of those numbers depending on the gender of the following noun.

There are two words for 100: **cem** for a round hundred and **cento** for anything over the hundred, eg. **102 bilhetes** (**cento e dois bilhetes**).

De interesse

Most Portuguese families sit under huge sunshades on the beach and take enormous picnics in cool boxes, so that a day on the beach is enjoyable and sunstroke-free!

13 People

Getting to know people

Vocabulário

como está?	how are you?
estou bem	I'm well
fala bem	you speak well
fala ...?	do you speak ...?
falo	I speak
não falo	I don't speak
um pouco (de)	a little, a bit (of)
português	Portuguese
francês	French
alemão	German

Diálogo

Anne Green	Boa tarde, Senhor Silva. Como está?
António da Silva	Boa tarde, Anne. Estou bem, obrigado. E a Anne? Como está?
Anne Green	Muito bem, obrigada.
António da Silva	A Anne fala bem português.
Anne Green	Obrigada. O senhor fala inglês?
António da Silva	Falo um pouco. Falo francês também. A Anne fala francês?
Anne Green	Não, não falo, mas falo um pouco de alemão.

Actividades

1 Tick or cross the languages each person does or does not speak.
(*Answers on page 127.*)

	French	English	Portuguese	German
1. Falo inglês, alemão e um pouco de francês.	☐	☐	☐	☐
2. Não falo francês, mas falo português bem.	☐	☐	☐	☐
3. Falo um pouco de alemão.	☐	☐	☐	☐

2 Listen to the people on the recording saying which languages they speak, and how well. Fill in their details on the table opposite. Put ** if they speak the language well, * if they speak a little, and – if no measure given. If they don't speak it, put a x. (*Answers on page 127.*)

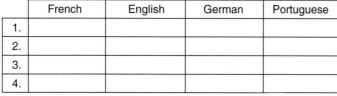

	French	English	German	Portuguese
1.				
2.				
3.				
4.				

3 Now take part in a dialogue, using the prompts below to guide you. Speak in the pauses. (*Answers on the recording and on page 127.*)

1. Hello, I'm well, thank you.
2. And how are you?
3. Thank you. Do you speak English?
4. I speak a bit of German, and also some French.

Língua

The nouns for the different languages are identical to the masculine word for nationalities. Therefore, **francês** can mean not only the French language but also a Frenchman. Most of the feminine forms will be composed by adding an **-a** to the masculine word, although there are a few exceptions.

male	*female*	*male plural*	*female plural*
francês	**francesa**	**franceses**	**francesas**
inglês	**inglesa**	**ingleses**	**inglesas**
português	**portuguesa**	**portugueses**	**portuguesas**
alemão	**alemã**	**alemães**	**alemãs**

Remember that all these words are also adjectives: **uma cidade inglesa** (an English city), **camisas alemãs** (German shirts).

De interesse

When people are on more friendly terms you will hear them refer to each other as **o/a + the person's name**. See the table below:

	formal	*informal*
masculine	**o senhor**	**o Luís**
feminine	**a senhora**	**a Anne**

Eating out

Making choices

Vocabulário

o que vão tomar?	what are you (pl.) going to have?
o que tem de sanduiches?	what have you got in sandwiches?
e para beber?	and to drink?
para mim	for me
para a senhora	for you/madam
quero	I'd like (lit. 'I want')
pode ser	it can be/it'll be
(um) chá com leite	tea with milk
(o) bolo de amêndoa	almond cake
(o) bolo de chocolate	chocolate cake
uma fatia de	a slice of
uma sanduiche/sandes	a sandwich
(o) queijo	cheese
(o) fiambre	ham
(o) ovo	egg
(o) atum	tuna

Diálogo

customer 1	Faz favor!
waiter	Bom dia, senhores. O que vão tomar?
customer 1	Bom, para mim é um chá com leite e uma fatia de bolo de amêndoa.
waiter	E para a senhora?
customer 2	O que tem de sanduiches?
waiter	De sandes temos queijo, fiambre, ovo e atum.
customer 2	Então quero uma de queijo, se faz favor.
waiter	E para beber?
customer 2	Para mim pode ser uma bica.

Actividades

1   Fill in the spaces with words from the boxes. (*Answers on page 127.*)

1. Para mim, ... um bica e uma .... de .... de amêndoa.

2. Para .... senhora, é um chá .... leite e uma .... de ovo.

3. Para José .... ser uma bica e .... sandes de queijo.

sanduiche	a	uma	fatia	bolo	pode	é	com

2   Listen to the speakers ordering in a café and decide whether the statements below are true (**verdadeiro**) or false (**falso**). (*Answers on page 127.*)

	V	F
Speaker **1** wants a ham sandwich and an espresso coffee.	☐	☐
Speaker **2** wants some chocolate cake and an egg sandwich.	☐	☐
Speaker **3** would like a white coffee and two tuna sandwiches.	☐	☐

3   Now take part in a dialogue in a café. Follow the prompts below. (*Answers on the recording and on page 127.*)

    1. For me, a small black coffee and a slice of chocolate cake.
    2. What have you got in sandwiches?
    3. Well, I'm going to have an egg one, please.

Língua

The word **é** is from the verb 'to be' (**ser**), and it means 'is'. You came across it earlier, in Unit 9. It is frequently used when ordering food and drink, instead of saying 'I'll have'. The Portuguese say 'for me, it's a …'.

De interesse

There is a variety of eating places in Portugal. There is the **café** (a word which means both 'coffee' and 'café') and there is also the **pastelaria**. Although this means literally 'the cake shop', these places mostly have tables for you to sit down and gorge yourself on the wonderful **bolos** and **pastéis**!

15 Accommodation

Reserving a room

Vocabulário

quer ...?	do you want ...?	**Janeiro**	January
reservar	to reserve	**Fevereiro**	February
para que dia?	for when/which day?	**Março**	March
pretende ficar	(do) you intend to stay	**Abril**	April
sem	without	**Maio**	May
a pousada	the state-run hotel/inn	**Junho**	June
a casa de banho	the bathroom	**Julho**	July
o pequeno almoço	the breakfast	**Agosto**	August
incluído	included	**Setembro**	September
		Outubro	October
		Novembro	November
		Dezembro	December

Diálogo

receptionist	Pousada dos Loios, bom dia.
customer	Bom dia. Queria reservar um quarto individual, se faz favor.
receptionist	Para que dia?
customer	Para o dia vinte e cinco de Maio.
receptionist	Quantas noites pretende ficar?
customer	Quatro.
receptionist	Quer com ou sem casa de banho?
customer	Com, se faz favor.

Actividades

1 Match the captions to the pictures. (*Answers on page 127.*)

1. Um quarto simples com casa de banho e pequeno almoço. **a)**

2. Um quarto de casal com casa de banho para três noites. **b)**

3. Um quarto individual sem casa de banho para uma noite. **c)**

4. Um quarto simples com casa de banho, sem pequeno almoço. **d)**

2 Listen to the customers on the tape reserving rooms in a **pousada** and tick on the table below what is required by each one. (*Answers on page 127.*)

	quarto		casa de banho		pequeno almoço	
	individual	casal	com	sem	incluído	não incluído
1.						
2.						

3 Now take part in a dialogue with a hotel receptionist. Follow the prompts below. (*Answers on the recording and on page 127.*)

   1. Good afternoon, I would like to reserve a double room.
   2. For the 27th January.
   3. Two.
   4. With, please.

Língua

The months are written in Portuguese with a capital first letter, except in Brazil.

De interesse

Pousadas are the Portuguese equivalent of the Spanish **paradores**. They are state-run luxury inns and hotels, usually located in beautiful old buildings, such as castles, monasteries and manor houses. Other forms of accommodation in Portugal include bed and breakfast (**pensão**), the guest house (**residência/residencial**), and the inn (**albergaria/estalagem**).

UNIT 16

Travel

A train journey

Vocabulário

quanto custa?	how much does it cost?	duzentos	200
de primeira classe	first class	trezentos	300
de segunda classe	second class	quatrocentos	400
uma nota	a note (monetary)	quinhentos	500
um conto	a 1,000 escudo note (colloquial)	seiscentos	600
o seu troco	your change	setecentos	700
		oitocentos	800
qual é ...?	which is ...?	novecentos	900
a linha	the platform	mil	1,000
qual é a linha?	which platform is it?		
o comboio	the train		
parte	it departs		
(a) partida	departure		
quanto tempo falta para?	how much time is there before?		
daqui a vinte minutos	in 20 minutes		

Diálogo

traveller	Faz favor, queria um bilhete de ida e volta para o Porto.
ticket clerk	De primeira ou segunda classe?
traveller	De segunda. Quanto custa?
ticket clerk	Dois mil trezentos e quarenta e cinco escudos.
traveller	Aqui tem uma nota de cinco mil.
ticket clerk	Cinco contos. Muito bem. Aqui está o seu troco.
traveller	Qual é a linha?
ticket clerk	O comboio parte da linha número seis.
traveller	Quanto tempo falta para a partida?
ticket clerk	O comboio parte daqui a vinte minutos.

Actividades

1 You have been sent shopping with a five-conto note
(**5,000 escudos**). Match up the items below with the correct
amounts of change you should receive after you buy them.
(*Answers on page 127.*)

1.   2.   3.   4.   5.

O seu troco:

a) Dois mil duzentos e cinquenta escudos.
b) Mil oitocentos e sessenta e cinco escudos.
c) Três contos trezentos e cinquenta e sete.
d) Dois contos cento e dez.
e) Oitocentos e oitenta escudos.

2 Listen to someone asking for train tickets and answer the following questions in English. (*Answers on page 127.*)

    1. First or second class?
    2. The train leaves from which platform?
    3. The price of the ticket is …?
    4. The train is due to leave in how many minutes?

3 Now take part in a dialogue yourself, based on the one on the opposite page. Use the prompts below to guide you. You start. (*Answers on the recording and on page 127.*)

    1. I'd like a return ticket to Braga, please.
    2. First class. How much does it cost?
    3. Which platform is it?

Língua

As you might have noticed, when a number in full is composed of up to three parts, each part is separated by an **e** (and): **vinte *e* um** (21), **cento *e* trinta *e* quatro** (134), **mil *e* quarenta *e* cinco** (1.045). Those composed of four parts or more, however, will not have **e** after the 'thousand', 'million' etc. Therefore: **mil, duzentos *e* trinta *e* quatro** (1.234), **vinte *e* um mil quinhentos *e* sessenta *e* sete** (21.567).

The numbers 200–900 also have a feminine form: '341 beers' is **trezent*as* e quarenta e um*a* cervejas**.

De interesse

If you need to change money in Portugal, the following vocabulary might be useful:

casa de câmbio	bureau de change	**compra**	buying
câmbio	currency exchange	**venda**	selling
cotação	rate of exchange	**moeda**	coin
		nota	note

17 Directions

Finding out where the bank is

Vocabulário

onde fica ...?	where is ...?
ora bem	well now
passa	(you) pass
por	through, by
pela	through, by the
ao lado de	next to
volta	(you) turn/return
para trás	back, round
atravessa	(you) cross
detrás de	behind
(o) museu	museum

Diálogo

visitor	Faz favor. Onde fica o banco?
man	Ora bem. A senhora vira aqui à esquerda, passa pela Praça São Vicente, e o banco fica ao lado do cinema.
visitor	Muito obrigada.
man	De nada.

visitor	Desculpe, onde fica a Praça São Vicente?
passer-by	A Praça São Vicente? Pois, a senhora volta para trás, atravessa a avenida, e a praça fica detrás do museu.

Actividades

1 Which bank are you looking for? Fill in the appropriate word(s) to indicate where each bank is located. (*Answers on page 127.*)

1. **2.** **3.** **4.**

a) O Banco Forte fica .... cinema.
b) O Banco Rico fica .... Camões.
c) O Banco d'Ouro fica .... museu.
d) O Banco Soares fica .... turismo

2 The Banco Gordo is in the Praça Municipal, next to the butchers. Listen to two people asking where the bank is and decide which one of them is given the true location. (*Answers on page 127.*)

	verdadeiro	falso
1.	☐	☐
2.	☐	☐

3 Take part in a dialogue as you try to find out where the bank is. You start. (*Answers on the recording and on page 127.*)

1. Where is the bank?
2. Excuse me, can you repeat that more slowly, please?
3. Is it very far?
4. Thank you very much.

Língua

In the dialogue we had another example of two words combining, or contracting: *pela* praça (through the square). This is a combination of the word **por** (by/through), plus **a** (the).

	singular		plural	
por	**+ o**	**+ a**	**+ os**	**+ as**
	pelo	**pela**	**pelos**	**pelas**

eg. **pelos parques**   through the parks
   pelas avenidas   through the avenues

De interesse

Museums in Portugal usually close on Mondays. Cinemas are very cheap and popular with all ages. Banks generally open from 8.30 until 3.30. Most offer a wide range of services, including **câmbio** (exchange), and in most large towns you will find automatic cash dispensers for use with credit cards.

Town amenities

At the bank

Vocabulário

trocar	to change
quantos …?	how many …?
libras esterlinas	pounds sterling
cada	each (one)
em total	in all
portanto	so, in that case
o seu, a sua	your
o passaporte	the passport
a morada	the address
(a) sua morada	your address
a chapa	the small disc (see **De interesse**)
assinar	to sign
leva	(you) take
para receber	(in order) to receive
à caixa	at, to the cash desk

Diálogo

visitor	Queria trocar estes travellers cheques, se faz favor.
bank clerk	Com certeza. Quantos tem?
visitor	Tenho dez cheques, de cinquenta libras cada.
bank clerk	Portanto, são quinhentas libras esterlinas em total. Tem o seu passaporte?
visitor	Aqui está.
bank clerk	Qual é a sua morada aqui em Portugal?
visitor	É o Hotel Miraflores, Avenida de São João, número vinte e quatro, Braga.
bank clerk	Faz o favor de assinar os cheques. A senhora leva esta chapa à caixa para receber o dinheiro.

Actividades

1 Match the captions to the pictures. (*Answers on page 127.*)

1. trezentas e cinquenta libras esterlinas   **a)**

2. um passaporte   **b)**

3. a morada em Portugal   **c)**

4. assinar os cheques **d)**

5. esta chapa **e)**

6. receber o dinheiro **f)**

2 Listen to someone at the bank and fill in the information from their transaction on the table below. (*Answers on page 127.*)

quantos cheques?	dinheiro em total	hotel name	hotel address

3 Take part in a dialogue in a bank, using the prompts below. You start. (*Answers on the recording and on page 127.*)

1. I'd like to change these travellers cheques.
2. Five, twenty pounds each one.
3. Here it is.
4. Hotel Palácio, Rua Principal, 36, Nazaré.

Língua

The form for 'your' depends on the gender and number of the word that follows, and not on the person doing the possessing. Therefore, you must know whether the possessed item is masculine, or feminine, singular or plural.

noun	your	example	
o dinheiro	(o) seu	(o) seu dinheiro	your money
a morada	(a) sua	(a) sua morada	your address
os bolos	(os) seus	(os) seus bolos	your cakes
as camisas	(as) suas	(as) suas camisas	your shirts

Note that it is possible and common to use the article 'the' (**o, a, os, as**) before possessive words in Portuguese.

De interesse

Not all banks in Portugal hand out **chapas**, but if you are handed a disc with a number on it, you need to go and wait where the sign says **caixa** (cashier) and listen for the number to be called so that you don't miss your turn to get your money.

The town centre

Buying clothes in the shopping centre

Vocabulário

uma loja de roupas	a clothes shop	**alguma coisa**	something
o centro comercial	the shopping centre/arcade	**vários/as**	various, several
uma blusa	a blouse	**aquela**	that (one)
o padrão	the style	**encontrar**	to find
a cor	the colour		
o tamanho	the size	**experimentar**	to try (on)
		levo	I'll take
verde	green	**custam**	they cost
amarelo	yellow		
cor-de-rosa	pink		

Diálogo

woman	Desculpe. Onde é que posso encontrar uma loja de roupas?
man	Pois, há várias aqui no centro comercial.
woman	Bom dia. Quero comprar uma blusa.
assistant	Temos vários padrões e cores. Qual é o seu tamanho?
woman	É o quarenta e dois. Tem alguma coisa em azul?
assistant	Temos esta em azul, esta em verde ou em amarelo, e temos aquela em cor-de-rosa.
woman	Posso experimentar estas duas?
assistant	Claro que pode.
woman	Quanto custa esta?
assistant	Mil e duzentos escudos.
woman	E aquela?
assistant	Mil, cento e noventa.
woman	Então levo esta. Obrigada.

Actividades

1 Match what the people are saying down the middle with the pictures on either side. (*Answers on page 127.*)

THIS ONE

a)

b)

AMARELO

c)

VERDE

1. Quero esta blusa verde.

2. Levo esta blusa, medida quarenta e dois.

3. Posso experimentar aquela blusa azul?

4. Quanto custa esta em amarelo?

5. Quero aquela no tamanho 42.

THAT ONE

d)

e)

AZUL

2 Listen to someone buying a blouse in a shop and write the details on the table below. (*Answers on page 127.*)

Size	blue	pink	green	yellow
colours shown?				
price of each?				
colour chosen?				

3 Now take part in a dialogue yourself, using the pictures below to prompt you. (*Answers on the recording and on page 127.*)

a)

1. Say what you'd like to buy. (a)

b)

2. Answer the question. (b)
Ask if there's anything in green.

c)

3. Ask to try on that one. (c)

4. Ask how much it costs.

THIS ONE   THAT ONE

Língua

Pointing things out.

	masculine	feminine		masculine	feminine
this	**este**	**esta**	these	**estes**	**estas**
that	**aquele**	**aquela**	those	**aqueles**	**aquelas**
	este bolo	this cake		**aquela blusa**	that blouse
	estas camisas	these shirts		**aqueles sapatos**	those shoes

De interesse

The shopping centres are becoming increasingly popular in larger Portuguese towns. The most famous is the huge **Centro Comercial Amoreiras** in Lisbon, which was a controversial departure in Portuguese architecture. There is now an even bigger one called the **Centro Comercial Colombo**. Remember that you will need to use continental sizes in Portugal. See the table below.

Ladies' dress sizes

UK	10	12	14	16	18
Portugal	38	40	42	44	46

Personal choices

When do you usually go shopping?

Vocabulário

sempre	always
nem sempre	not always
geralmente	generally
em geral	generally
de vez em quando	sometimes
às vezes	sometimes
muitas vezes	often
poucas vezes	little (seldom)
quase nunca	hardly ever
aos fins de semana	at the weekend(s)
nas terças	on Tuesdays
fazer as compras	to do the/go shopping
fazes as compras	you do the/go shopping
faço	I do, make
vou	I go
vais	(do) you go
gostas de ir	you like to go
ando muito ocupado/a	I'm very busy
o supermercado	the supermarket
o mercado	the market
a feira	the monthly (gypsy) market
uma pechincha	a bargain
tu	you (familiar)

Diálogo

João Olá, Maria, boa tarde. Então, sempre fazes as compras nas terças?

Maria Nem sempre, João. Geralmente vou ao supermercado nas segundas, mas esta semana ando muito ocupada.

João Pessoalmente, prefiro fazer as compras aos fins de semana, mas de vez em quando vou nas quartas. Vais muitas vezes ao mercado?

Maria Em geral faço as compras no mercado três vezes por semana. Às vezes vou à feira – sempre há uma pechincha. E tu, João, quando é que gostas de ir à feira?

João À feira, pois, poucas vezes, quase nunca. Gosto mais do centro comercial.

Actividades

1 Match up the Portuguese and English phrases. (*Answers on page 127.*)

1. Às vezes vou ao supermercado.
2. Nunca vou à feira.
3. Vou ao mercado, em geral.
4. Vou muitas vezes à feira.
5. Sempre faço as compras no mercado.

a) Generally I go to the market.
b) Sometimes I go to the supermarket.
c) I often go to the monthly market.
d) I never go to the monthly market.
e) I always shop at the market.

2 Listen to Paula and José talking about their shopping habits and write down on the table how often they go to the places below. (*Answers on page 127.*)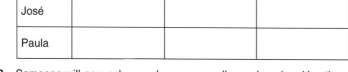

	market	supermarket	monthly market
José			
Paula			

3 Someone will now ask you when you usually go shopping. Use the prompts below to guide you. (*Answers on the recording and on page 127.*)

1. Not always, sometimes I go shopping in the supermarket.
2. I hardly ever go to the monthly market.
3. Generally, I shop there on Thursdays, but this week I'm very busy.

Língua

Up to now, you have learned verb forms and forms of address in polite terms, using either **o/a senhor/a**, or **o/a + the person's name**. If you know someone well, or if you are talking to a member of your family or a young person, you can be less formal, and call them **tu** (you), as you will see in the dialogue on the opposite page. The verb forms are also different: apart from some irregulars, the **tu** form adds an **-s** to the polite form.

verb		polite form	familiar form
gostar	like	**gosta**	**gostas**
ir	go	**vai**	**vais**
fazer	make, do	**faz**	**fazes**

De interesse

The **feiras** are very popular in Portugal. They are generally monthly markets, selling everything from pots and baskets to clothes and farming utensils, as well as the usual food produce. Often moving from one village to another throughout the month, the Algarve **feiras** are generally run by gypsies and are colourful shopping grounds.

Holidays

Where and when do you spend your holidays?

Vocabulário

onde costumas ...?	where do you usually ...?
ir de férias	to go on holidays
passo	I spend
tiro	I take (holidays)
vou para ...	I go to ...
viajar	to travel
passear	to visit, stroll, wander
(n)a primavera	(in) spring
(n)o verão	(in) summer
(n)o inverno	(in) winter
(n)o outono	(in) autumn
a paisagem	the scenery
o campo	the countryside
a costa	the coast
a Suíça	Switzerland
a Grécia	Greece
a França	France
o Japão	Japan
a Alemanha	Germany
Portugal	Portugal
lindo	pretty
calmo	quiet, calm
fresco	cool, fresh

Diálogo

Joana Olá, Pedro! Então, vais de férias outra vez?

Pedro Sempre tiro as férias no inverno.

Joana Onde costumas passar as férias?

Pedro Em geral, passo as férias de inverno na Suíça porque a paisagem é muito linda.

Joana Prefiro viajar no outono quando o campo está mais calmo. Vou muitas vezes para a Grécia ou, de vez em quando, para a França.

Pedro E no verão, Joana, não gostas de viajar?

Joana Nunca tiro férias no verão – gosto mais de passear na costa, onde está mais fresco. E tu, Pedro?

Pedro Gosto de visitar o Japão, a Alemanha, ou Portugal, claro!

Actividades

1 For each statement opposite, write down in English when and where the people prefer to go on holiday. The first one is an example for you.
(*Answers on page 127.*)

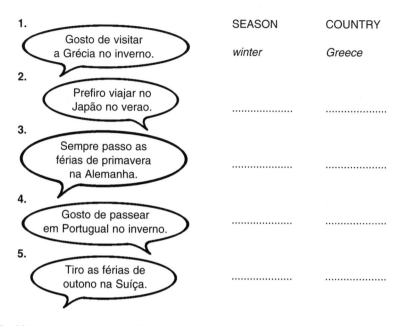

	SEASON	COUNTRY
1. Gosto de visitar a Grécia no inverno.	*winter*	*Greece*
2. Prefiro viajar no Japão no verao.	....	....
3. Sempre passo as férias de primavera na Alemanha.	....	....
4. Gosto de passear em Portugal no inverno.	....	....
5. Tiro as férias de outono na Suíça.	....	....

2 Listen to someone being interviewed about their holidays, and fill in the table below with their destinations. (*Answers on page 127.*)

spring	summer	autumn	winter

3 Now it's your turn to talk about holidays. Follow the prompts below and take part in the dialogue. (*Answers on the recording and on page 127.*)

1. I spend the spring holidays in France because the scenery is very pretty.
2. I never go on holiday in the summer.
3. In the autumn I like to visit Portugal, when the coast is quieter.

Língua

Countries' names are either masculine or feminine, and are mostly used with the appropriate **o/a** before them. One of the exceptions is Portugal itself, which does not use **o** or **a**. Further countries you may want to make a note of include:

os Estados Unidos	the USA	**a Inglaterra**	England
a Dinamarca	Denmark	**o País de Gales**	Wales
o Brasil	Brazil	**a Escócia**	Scotland
a Espanha	Spain	**a Irlanda**	Ireland

De interesse

Most Portuguese people take their holidays in the summer. The Algarve and the northern coastline (**Costa da Prata**) are very popular with Portuguese from the north.

The weather

Talking about bad weather

Vocabulário

(as) castanhas	chestnuts
um pacote	a packet
(o) ano	year
o mau tempo	the bad weather
(a) chuva	rain
(a) neve	snow
faz frio	it's cold
nublado	cloudy
quente	hot
razoável	reasonable
péssimo	terrible
normal	normal
estranho	strange
como	as/like
hoje em dia	nowadays
pois(é)	that's right
que bom	(how) good/lovely
tem razão	you're right

Diálogo

chestnut vendor	Castanhas quentes! Castanhas quentes!
woman	Que bom! Um pacote, se faz favor. Que mau tempo temos.
chestnut vendor	Tem razão. Hoje está um dia péssimo. Faz muito frio e o céu está nublado.
woman	Mas este tempo é normal aqui no inverno?
chestnut vendor	Não muito, não. Em geral temos tempo razoável, mas este ano há mais chuva e vento.
woman	Como na Inglaterra também. Hoje em dia o tempo é estranho.
chestnut vendor	Pois é.

Actividades

1   Match up the Portuguese and English weather expressions. (*Answers on page 127.*)

1. Faz frio.	**a)** It's snowing.
2. O céu está nublado.	**b)** It's cold.
3. Há neve.	**c)** It's raining.
4. Há chuva.	**d)** The sky is cloudy.
5. Há muito vento.	**e)** It's very windy.

2 Listen to these descriptions of the weather in two Portuguese cities, and decide which picture relates to each city. (*Answers on page 127.*)

1.

   ....

2.

   ....

3 Now take part in a dialogue about bad weather. Follow the prompts below. (*Answers on the recording and on page 127.*)

1. Good, I'll have two packets, please.
2. You're right. It's cold and cloudy.
3. Sometimes, but this year there is more wind.
4. Today is a terrible day for the beach.

Língua

Pois é, like the word **pois** on its own, is extremely common in Portuguese conversations, as a stopgap. It can mean: 'that's right', 'that's it', 'well', 'yes', or even just 'mmm!'.

De interesse

In some regions, such as the flat expanse of land in the middle of the country, the **Alentejo**, or the hilly **Trás-os-Montes** in the north, the temperature can drop below freezing. In the **Algarve** the weather is temperamental in the winter: some people have enjoyed Christmas on the beach, whilst for other visitors umbrellas and raincoats have been the order of the day.

III health

Getting a cold

Diálogo

woman	Aachoo!
man	Saúde!
woman	Obrigada! Estou um pouco constipada. Acho que é por causa da mudança do clima.
man	Provavelmente. Coitada! Estás a tomar algum remédio?
woman	Sim, estou a tomar aspirina porque também tenho uma dor de cabeça.
man	Não seria melhor ir descansar um pouco?
woman	Boa ideia! Também tenho uma dor de garganta. Vou tomar um xarope e vou para a cama. Estou muito cansada.

Actividades

1 Complete the speech bubbles, then match each one to a suggested remedy. (*Answers on page 127.*)

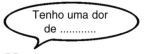

Tenho uma dor de ....

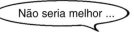

Não seria melhor ...

1.

a) tomar um xarope?

2. Tenho uma dor de ....

b) ir para a cama?

3. Aachoo! Estou ....

c) tomar uma aspirina?

2 Listen to the following dialogue between two people who are suffering from colds. Which speaker (male or female) has the sore throat? (*Answer on page 127.*)

3 Now take part in a dialogue about cold symptoms, following the prompts below. Start with a sneeze, then speak in the pauses. (*Answers on the recording and on page 127.*)

   1. Thanks, I've got a cold.
   2. I'm taking aspirin because I have a headache.
   3. Good idea. I also have a sore throat and I'm very tired.

Língua

If you want to say you are doing something currently, or if you want to ask someone about their current actions, Portuguese uses the construction **estar + a + infinitive**, which equates to the English '-ing' form.

Está a tomar ...?	Are you taking ...?
Sim, estou a tomar ...	Yes, I'm taking ...
Estamos a falar.	We are talking.
Tu estás a passear.	You are strolling.

De interesse

When you go to the chemist's in Portugal you will find most of the medication you are used to at home; in any case, the pharmacists are very helpful and will guide you towards the nearest equivalent medicine they have.

Time

Opening and closing times

Diálogo

tourist	Desculpe, sabe a que horas abre a farmácia?
woman	Há uma farmácia aqui que abre às oito e meia da manhã.
tourist	E a que horas fecha?
woman	Fecha à uma para o almoço. Depois, reabre às três e um quarto, e fecha às seis menos dez.
tourist	Preciso duma farmácia agora.
woman	Há uma farmácia de urgência mesmo ali, que abre das sete menos um quarto até às oito e vinte.
tourist	Obrigado.

Actividades

1 Match up the captions with the opening or closing times of the shops below. (*Answers on page 127.*)

1. Abre às dez menos um quarto da manhã.   **a)**

> Banco Real
> 8.15 am–4.15 pm

2. Abre às oito e um quarto da manhã.   **b)**

> Talho Bom
> 8.00 am–4.35 pm

3. Fecha às nove e meia.   **c)**

> Loja de Roupas Finas
> 10.30 am–9.30 pm

4. Fecha às cinco menos vinte e cinco.

d)
> Livraria Cultural
> 9.45 am–6.45 pm

5. Abre às oito menos vinte.

e)
> Pastelaria Sabor
> 7.40 am–10.00 pm

2 Listen to two people asking about opening and closing times of different places, and fill in the missing information on the table below. (*Answers on page 127.*)

	place	opens	closes	lunch hour
1.	museum			
2.		7.00 am		

3 Now imagine someone asks you about the opening times of the local bank. Use the signs below to guide you and take part in a dialogue on the tape. (*Answers on the recording and on page 127.*)

1. 8.20–12.30 Aberto
2. ALMOÇO
3. 1.15–3.45 Aberto

Língua

Time

at 1.00	à uma (hora)
at 2.00	às duas (horas)
at 12.00	às doze horas
at midday	ao meio-dia
at midnight	à meia-noite
at 3.10	às três (horas) e dez (minutos)
at 4.15	às quatro (horas) e quinze (minutos)
	às quatro e um quarto
at 5.30	às cinco (horas) e trinta (minutos)
	às cinco e meia
at 6.40	às seis (horas) e quarenta (minutos)
	às sete menos vinte
	aos vinte para as sete
at 7.45	às sete (horas) e quarenta e cinco (minutos)
	às oito menos um quarto
	a um quarto para as oito

On timetables, the 24-hour clock is used, therefore:
21.32   vinte e uma (horas) e trinta e dois (minutos)

De interesse

Most shops in Portugal close from 1.00 to 3.00 pm, and then open until 7.00 or 8.00 in the evening. In some shopping centres they stay open until 10.00 or 11.00 pm. Restaurants seem to stay open until everyone has finished enjoying themselves!

People

Talking about families

Vocabulário

apresentar	to introduce
(o) marido	husband
(a) mulher	wife
o meu marido	my husband
a minha mulher	my wife
o marido dela	her husband
(o) pai	father
(os) pais	parents
(a) mãe	mother
(o) irmão	brother
(a) irmã	sister
(os) irmãos	brothers; brothers and sisters
(o) filho	son
(a) filha	daughter
(os) filhos	children
(a) família	family
casado/a	married
solteiro/a	single
simpático/a	nice, kind
sueco	Swedish
a Suécia	Sweden
ainda	still
vive	lives
vivem	they live
tem saudades da família?	do you miss your family?

Diálogo

António da Silva	Olá, Anne. Queria apresentar a minha mulher, Maria da Graça.
Anne Green	Muito prazer.
Maria da Graça da Silva	Igualmente. A Anne é casada?
Anne Green	Não, não sou. Ainda sou solteira.
António da Silva	Mas tem família?
Anne Green	Claro. Na minha família há o meu pai, a minha mãe, eu e …
António da Silva	Não tem irmãos?
Anne Green	Sim, tenho. Tenho um irmão que vive nos Estados Unidos. É casado e tem três filhos – um filho e duas filhas. Também tenho uma irmã. O marido dela é sueco. Vivem na Suécia.
António da Silva	Tem saudades da família?
Anne Green	Tenho, mas os portugueses são muito simpáticos.

Actividades

1   Complete the sentences opposite about this Portuguese family. Choose from the words opposite. (*Answers on page 127.*)

| os filhos | a irmã | o marido | a filha | casados | a mãe | o irmão |

| o filho | a mulher | o pai |

Júlia   Paulo

Pedro   Ana   Maria

1. A Júlia é .... do Paulo.
2. O Paulo e a Júlia são ....
3. O Paulo é .... da Júlia.
4. A Júlia é .... do Pedro, da Ana e da Maria.
5. O Paulo é .... do Pedro, da Ana e da Maria.
6. A Pedro é .... da Júlia.
7. A Ana é .... do Paulo.
8. A Maria, o Pedro e a Ana são .... da Júlia e do Paulo.
9. A Maria é .... do Pedro.
10. O Pedro é .... da Ana.

2 Listen to two people describing their closest family and fill in their details on the table below. Write down how many children, brothers and/or sisters they have. (*Answers on page 128.*)

	married	children	brothers	sisters
1.				
2.				

3 Using the **Língua** notes below, give the Portuguese translation for the following sentences. (*Answers on the recording and on page 128.*)

1. He speaks English.   **2.** Do you (polite, masculine) live in Sweden?
3. They (feminine) are called Mary and Jean.   **4.** His brother lives in France.
5. Her husband is called José.

Língua

In this unit you are introduced to a verb in the plural, ie. describing the actions of more than one person. In most cases the pattern from singular to plural form in the present is like this:

verb		he/she/you (polite)	they/you (pl.)
falar	to speak	fala	falam
chamar-se	to be called	chama-se	chamam-se
viver	to live	vive	vivem
abrir	to open	abre	abrem

The subjects of the verbs (those doing the action) can be expressed by means of the following pronouns:

I	you	he	she	you	we	you	they
eu	tu	ele	ela	o/a senhor/a	nós	os/as senhores/as	eles/elas
	(familiar)			(polite)		(pl.)	(masc./fem.)

his/her can be conveyed by saying 'the … of he/she':

o marido dela	her husband (lit. 'the husband of she')
a mulher dele	his wife (lit. 'the wife of he')
O marido dela é sueco	Her husband is Swedish.

De interesse

Portuguese families are generally quite large, although not as large as they used to be.

Eating out

Ordering a meal for two

Vocabulário

vão querer ...?	are you going to want ...?
para começar	to start (with)
e depois?	and then?
(a) lista	menu
(uma) sopa de agriões	watercress soup
(um) caldo verde	shredded kale soup
(a) carne de porco à alentejana	pork and clams Alentejo-style
(um) bacalhau à Brás	cod with eggs and potatoes
(a) sopa de legumes	vegetable soup
(o) frango piri-piri	chicken piri-piri
(as) sardinhas assadas	grilled sardines
(o) leitão assado	roast sucking pig
(as) sobremesas	desserts
(a) mousse de chocolate	chocolate mousse
(o) arroz doce	rice pudding (cold)
(o) pudim	crème caramel
(a) salada de frutas	fruit salad
(os) papos de anjo	egg-based sweet dessert
(a) baunilha	vanilla
(uma) garrafa	bottle
(o) vinho da casa	house wine
tinto	red
branco	white

Diálogo

customer	A lista, se faz favor.
waiter	Com certeza.

waiter	Diga, se faz favor.
customer	Para começar, é uma sopa de agriões e um caldo verde.
waiter	Muito bem, e depois?
customer	Para mim, pode ser a carne de porco à alentejana e, para o meu marido, um bacalhau à Brás.
waiter	Vão querer sobremesas?
customer	O que tem?
waiter	Hoje há mousse de chocolate, arroz doce, pudim, salada de frutas e papos de anjo.
customer	Então pode ser um pudim e uma mousse.
waiter	E para beber?
customer	Uma garrafa do vinho da casa.
waiter	Tinto ou branco?
customer	Tinto. Obrigada.

Actividades

1 Match the captions to the pictures. (*Answers on page 128.*)

1. uma salada de frutas
2. duas sopas
3. a lista
4. uma garrafa de vinho branco
5. duas garrafas de vinho tinto

a)   b)   c)   d)   e)

2 Look at the menu for the Restaurante Imperial and listen to Mr and Mrs Gomes ordering a meal. Tick the food and drink they order. (*Answers on page 128.*)

RESTAURANTE IMPERIAL

Hoje há

Sopa de legumes
Sopa de agriões
Caldo verde

Mousse de chocolate
Bolo de amêndoa
Gelados – morango
　　　　 – baunilha
　　　　 – chocolate

Bacalhau à Brás
Carne de porco à alentejana
Frango piri-piri
Sardinhas assadas
Leitão assado

Vinho de casa – tinto
　　　　　　 – branco

3 Now see if you can order a meal for yourself and your brother. Use the prompts below to guide you and, if necessary, refer to the menu above. You start. (*Answers on the recording and on page 128.*)

1. The menu, please.　　2. To start with, one kale soup and one vegetable soup.
3. For me, the grilled sardines and, for my brother, the cod.　　4. What is there?
5. Two fruit salads.　　6. A bottle of house wine.　　7. Red, thanks.

Língua

Vão is another example of a verb in the plural, this time from the irregular verb **ir** (to go). Here is the present tense in full:

eu	**vou**	(I go)	nós	**vamos**	(we go)
tu	**vais**	(You go)	os srs/as sras	**vão**	(You pl. go)
ele/ela	**vai**	(He/She/it goes)	eles/elas	**vão**	(They go).
o sr/a sra	**vai**	(you go - *formal*)			

De interesse

Portuguese cuisine is well-known for its heartiness and delicious combinations of olive oil (**azeite de oliva**), garlic (**alho**) and spices (**temperos**) such as piri-piri, brought back from far-off places by the navigators of old. It is also rather salty. Pork (**carne de porco**) is always a good choice, as is fish (**peixe**). The Portuguese eat a huge range of fish, the most famous being the typical salted cod – **o bacalhau**.

Accommodation

Checking into a campsite reservation

Vocabulário

(vocês) têm …?	do you (pl.) have …?
um lugar	a place
(a) tenda	the tent
(a) caravana	the caravan
(o) carro-cama	the campervan
(a) vaga	the pitch/site
ao fundo de	at the far end of
(o) parque	the park, campsite
(a) ficha	the form
(o) nome	the first name
(o) apelido	the surname
(a) data	the date
(o) nascimento	the birth
(o) local de nascimento	the place of birth
(a) chegada	the arrival
(a) recepção	the reception desk
já está	it's done, there
faz favor de	please
preencher	to fill in
reservado	reserved
em que nome?	in what name?

Diálogo

customer	Bom dia. Temos um lugar reservado.
receptionist	Em que nome?
customer	Brown.
receptionist	Ah, sim, aqui está. Vocês têm tenda, caravana, ou carro-cama?
customer	Uma caravana e uma tenda.
receptionist	Está bem. O número da vaga é o vinte e dois. Fica à esquerda, ao fundo do parque. Agora, faz favor de preencher esta ficha.
customer	Claro. O que precisa saber?
receptionist	O seu nome, apelido, número do passaporte, local e data de nascimento, a sua morada, e a data de chegada ao parque.
customer	Já está.
receptionist	A recepção fecha às dez e meia da noite e abre às sete horas da manhã.
customer	Obrigado.

Actividades

1 Fill in the form opposite with the appropriate pieces of information. (*Answers on page 128.*)

dos Santos Pereira	Rua S. Pedro, 10, 3°esq, Braga	português

Castelo Branco	BI 372201568BJL	terça-feira, 10 de Junho de 1998

José	25 de Março de 1963

> **Parque de Campismo Belavista**
>
> Nome ....
> Apelido ....
> Data de nascimento ....
> Local de nascimento ....
> Morada ....
> N° de passaporte/bilhete de identidade ....
> Nacionalidade ....
> Data de chegada ....

2 Listen to someone checking in at a campsite. Look at the plan of the site below, and mark on it where they are placed, and whether they have a tent (T), caravan (C), or campervan (CV). (*Answers on page 128.*)

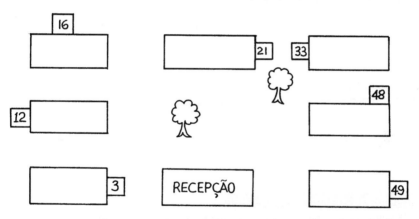

3 Somebody will ask you for some personal information. Try to answer each question in a natural way. Speak in the pauses on the recording. (*Answers on page 128.*)

Língua

When addressing more than one person, in less formal situations, an alternative to **os senhores/as senhoras** is **vocês** ('you' – pl.). You can, of course, simply use the plural verb form, as you have seen in recent units, but as that form is also used for 'they', the use of **vocês** makes it clear who is doing the action. The singular equivalent is **você**, which is used widely throughout Brazil and by some people in Portugal.

De interesse

In Portugal each person has an ID card – **um bilhete de identidade (BI)**.

Travel

A coach journey

Vocabulário

uma camioneta	a coach
partem	they depart
de 30 em 30 minutos	every 30 minutes
de meia em meia hora	every half an hour
a próxima	the next one
é directa?	is it direct?
tem de	you have to
mudar	to change
chega	arrives
uma paragem	a rest, stop
breve	short, brief

Diálogo

traveller	A que horas há uma camioneta para Évora?
ticket clerk	As camionetas para Évora partem de trinta em trinta minutos.
traveller	Bom, de meia em meia hora. E a que horas parte a próxima?
ticket clerk	A próxima para Évora parte às dezassete e vinte e cinco.
traveller	É directa?
ticket clerk	Não. A senhora tem de mudar em Portalegre. A camioneta chega às dezoito e quarenta e cinco. Há uma breve paragem de quinze minutos. Parte às dezanove horas e chega a Évora às vinte e trinta.
traveller	Então, queria um bilhete de ida e volta, se faz favor.
ticket clerk	Aqui só pode comprar a ida. O bilhete de volta tem de comprar lá, antes de viajar. Ora bem, são dois mil quinhentos e cinquenta escudos.

Actividades

1   Fill in the gaps in this exercise, using the timetable to guide you.
   (*Answers on page 128.*)

Camionetas para										
Braga	8.00	8.45	9.30	10.15	11.00	11.45	12.30	13.15	14.00	14.45
Évora	8.15	8.30	8.45	9.00	9.15	9.30	9.45	10.00	10.15	10.30
Lisboa	8.25	8.50	9.15	9.40	10.05	10.30	10.55	11.20	11.45	12.10
Porto	8.30	9.20	10.10	11.00	11.50	12.40	13.30	14.20	15.10	16.00

a) As camionetas para o Porto partem de *cinquenta* em *cinquenta* minutos.

b) As camionetas para Évora partem de .... em .... minutos.

c) As camionetas para em .... partem de vinte e cinco em vinte e cinco minutos.

d) As camionetas para .... partem de quarenta e cinco em quarenta e cinco minutos.

2 Listen to a dialogue about a coach journey and fill in the table below with any missing information. (*Answers on page 128.*)

destination	how often	next departure	change	arrival at destination

3 Now take part in a dialogue based on the one on the opposite page. (*Answers on the recording and on page 128.*)

1. What time is there a coach to Viana?
2. And what time does the next one depart?
3. Is it direct?
4. How much does a ticket cost?

Língua

Ter de/que + infinitive   means 'to have to' (the verb **ter** means 'to have').

Temos de comprar vinho.   We have to buy wine.
Tenho que visitar Portugal.   I have to visit Portugal.

De interesse

When travelling by coach, you will usually be able to buy only single tickets. So you must allow time before your return to buy another ticket. All travel in Portugal is extremely cheap and there are luxury **rápido-expresso** coaches between the main cities, from Oporto down through Lisbon and to Faro in the Algarve.

Directions

Getting to the right platform

Vocabulário

sai	(it) leaves
para chegar lá?	to get there? (how does one get there?)
suba	go up
passe (por)	pass (by, through, over)
desça	go down
vire	turn
continue	continue
tome	take
espere	wait
vamos?	shall we go?
sempre em frente	right ahead
as escadas	the steps
a passarela	the footbridge
a bilheteira	the ticket office
lá em cima	up there
um momento	a moment
já	already
perdido/a	lost
gentil	kind
fácil	easy
assim	that way
consigo	with you
ora essa!	the very idea, come off it!

Diálogo

visitor	Desculpe. O comboio para Faro sai de que linha?
man	Da linha número três.
visitor	E para chegar lá?
man	Pois, suba estas escadas aqui, passe pela passarela lá em cima e desça até ao quiosque. Depois, vire à esquerda, continue sempre em frente até à bilheteira e tome a primeira à …
visitor	Espere um momento, já estou perdida!
man	Então vou lá consigo. Assim é mais fácil.
visitor	O senhor é muito gentil.
man	Ora essa! Vamos?

Actividades

1   Match the pictures to the directions. (*Answers on page 128.*)

 a) passe

 b) suba

1.

2.

 c) desça **d)** lá em cima

3.

4.

 e) continue sempre em frente

5.

2 Listen to someone being given instructions to get to the correct platform. Note down the directions you hear and the correct platform number. (*Answers on page 128.*)

Directions: ....

....

....

Platform number:..

3 Now take part in a dialogue at a station. You want to know from where the train for Braga leaves. Follow the prompts below and see if you fully understand all the directions you are given. (*Answers on the recording and on page 128.*)

1. From which platform does the train to Braga leave?
2. How do I get there?
3. Hang on a second. I'm already lost!
4. You're very kind, thank you.

Língua

When giving someone directions, you can tell them what to do in a couple of ways: by saying 'you do this' as a suggestion, or simply 'do this', as a polite command.

Verb		Suggestion		Polite Command (o/a senhor/a …)	
passar	to pass	**passa**	you pass	**passe!**	pass!
virar	to turn	**vira**	you turn	**vire!**	turn!
continuar	to continue	**continua**	you continue	**continue!**	continue!
tomar	to take	**toma**	you take	**tome!**	take!
esperar	to wait for	**espera**	you wait	**espere!**	wait!
entrar	to enter	**entra**	you enter	**entre!**	enter!
descer	to go down	**desce**	you go down	**desça!**	go down!
ir	to go	**vai**	you go	**vá!**	go!
subir	to go up	**sobe**	you go up	**suba!**	go up!
seguir	to carry on	**segue**	you carry you	**siga!**	carry on!
sair	to leave	**sai**	you leave	**saia!**	leave

De interesse

Most train stations in Portugal, however small they are, have a bar or café serving hot and cold drinks, and snacks for your journey.

 # Town amenities

At the post office

Vocabulário

um selo	a stamp
(a) cabine	telephone booth
(uma) chamada	phone call
chamadas internacionais	international calls
chamada a cobrar	reverse charge (call)
no destino	at the receiving end (destination)
(o) país	country
(o) indicativo	code
(o) telefone	telephone
com quem	with whom
não desligue	don't hang up
qual ...?	which ...?
que ...?	what ...?

Diálogo

customer	Quanto custa um selo para a Inglaterra?
assistant	São oitenta escudos cada.
customer	Queria dez, se faz favor.
assistant	São oitocentos escudos. Quer mais alguma coisa?
customer	Queria fazer uma chamada.
assistant	Pode entrar na cabine três.
operator	Chamadas Internacionais, bom dia.
customer	Queria fazer uma chamada a cobrar no destino.
operator	Para que país?
customer	Inglaterra.
operator	Qual é o indicativo da cidade?
customer	É zero, um, cinco, dois, quatro.
operator	E o número do telefone?
customer	É quatro, dois, um, cinco, zero, seis.
operator	Com quem quer falar?
customer	Com a senhora White.
operator	E qual é o seu nome?
customer	David White.
operator	Está bem. Só um momento – não desligue.

Actividades

1 Match up the sets of stamps bought to the total amounts, and then work out what your change would be in each case if you paid with a **conto** (1,000 escudos). Write the full amounts in Portuguese. (*Answers on page 128.*)

1. 10 × 85esc

2. 7 × 110 esc

3. $4 \times$    **4.** $5 \times$

5. $2 \times$  $+$ $3 \times$

a) Quinhentos escudos
b) Oitocentos e cinquenta escudos
c) Quatrocentos e setenta e cinco escudos
d) Setecentos e setenta escudos
e) Quatrocentos e quarenta e cinco escudos

2 Listen to someone making an international call via an operator and fill in the table below with their details. (*Answers on page 128.*)

country	local code	telephone	wants to speak to

3 Now practise making an international call yourself. Use the dialogue opposite to guide you, and speak in the pauses, giving your own details. (*Answers on the recording and on page 128.*)

Língua

Many question words (interrogatives) in Portuguese begin with **qu**. You already know these:

quem?	**qual?**	**(o) que?**	**quando?**	**quanto?**
who?	which/what?	what?	when?	how much?

De interesse

Making phone calls in Portugal is very expensive, be it from **uma cabine telefônica** in the street, from the post office (**os correios**), or from the Telecom offices (**Telecomunicações Portuguesas**). Coin boxes are the most common, though card phones are becoming more widespread. You can buy the cards where you see the sign '**Cartão Credifone**'.

The town centre

Shopping at the market

Vocabulário

(os) tomates	tomatoes
(as) maçãs	apples
(as) batatas	potatoes
(as) laranjas	oranges
(a) couve-flor	cauliflower
(os) cogumelos	mushrooms
(as) cenouras	carrots
uma alface	a lettuce
a pera	the pear(s)
um melão	a melon
(o) que mais?	what else?
a como é …?	what price is …?
dê-me	give me
um quilo	a kilo
meio quilo	half a kilo
(os) gramas	grammes
maduro(s)	ripe

 ### Diálogo

customer	Bom dia, senhora. Tem tomates hoje?
vendor	Tenho, sim. Quantos quer? Estão muito bons hoje.
customer	Dê-me um quilo dos mais maduros.
vendor	Mais alguma coisa?
customer	Também queria um quilo de maçãs, cinco quilos de batatas, e dois de laranjas.
vendor	Que mais?
customer	Tem couve-flor?
vendor	Hoje não. Tenho cogumelos e cenouras.
customer	Dê-me duzentos e cinquenta gramas de cogumelos, se faz favor. Ah, e uma alface.
vendor	Mais?
customer	A como é a pera?
vendor	A trezentos o quilo.
customer	Então dê-me meio quilo, e também um melão, obrigado.

Actividades

1   Match the captions to the pictures. (*Answers on page 128.*)

1. um quilo de cenouras

a)

2. meio quilo de tomates   **b)**

3. duas alfaces   **c)**

4. duzentos e cinquenta gramas de cogumelos   **d)**

5. dois quilos de batatas   **e)**

2 Look at the list of market stall produce below, then listen to someone buying fruit and vegetables from it. Tick anything they buy, and write down how much they take. Cross out anything not available today. (*Answers on page 128.*)

1. tomatoes	**2.** potatoes	**3.** apples	**4.** oranges	**5.** cauliflower
6. mushrooms	**7.** carrots	**8.** lettuce	**9.** pears	**10.** melons
11. leeks	**12.** grapes	**13.** bananas	**14.** onions	**15.** plums

3 Now see if you can do your market shopping successfully. Take part in the dialogue, using the following prompts to guide you. (*Answers on the recording and on page 128.*)

1. Good morning. Do you have any mushrooms today?   **2.** I'll have 250g.
3. I'd also like $\frac{1}{2}$ kg of pears, 3 lettuces and 6 kg of potatoes.   **4.** Do you have any melons?   **5.** Well, then, give me a kilo of apples.   **6.** How much are the oranges today?   **7.** Give me 2 kg, thank you.

Língua

If metric weights still confuse you, the following approximations might help when you are buying foodstuffs.

	$2\frac{1}{2}$ kg	1 kg	$\frac{1}{2}$ kg	250g	100g
approx.	5 lbs	2 lbs	1 lb	$\frac{1}{2}$ lb	$\frac{1}{4}$ lb

To ask how much a product costs today, use **a como é o/a** …?. The answer will be **a … o quilo** (ie. 'x escudos *the* kilo', not '*a* kilo').
To say 'of the best/ripest/cheapest', etc, remember the contacted forms of **dos** and **das** you learned in Unit 5:

     um quilo *dos* mais baratos = a kilo of the cheapest

De interesse

Fresh fruit and vegetables are very cheap in Portugal, especially when bought at the **mercado**. Try the delicious oranges, tasty tomatoes, and refreshing melons.

Personal choices

What would you like to do?

Vocabulário

o que (é que) …?	what (is it that) …?
(tu) gostarias	you would like
gostaria	I would like
preferias	you would prefer
preferia	I would prefer
(eu) sempre quis	I've always wanted
(eu) sei	I know
fechado(s)	closed
concordas	(do) you agree
concordo	I agree
jantamos	we dine
passear	to stroll
podemos	we can
jantar	to dine
relaxar	to relax
tens razão	you're right
fica combinado	that's decided then
amanhã	tomorrow
já que	given that, as
(o) feriado	national holiday
fora	out, outside
em casa	at home
mais tarde	later
por fim	finally
comigo	with me
nesse caso	in that case
um filme	a film
um bar	a bar
uma boate	a nightclub

Diálogo

Maria Então, João, o que é que tu gostarias de fazer amanhã?

João Bom, já que amanhã é feriado, gostaria de ir ver um filme ao cinema, depois jantar fora, e por fim relaxar num bar.

Maria Não preferias visitar o Museu dos Coches comigo? Eu sempre quis ir.

João Todos os museus estão fechados nos feriados.

Maria Tens razão. Nesse caso preferia passear pela avenida, tomar uma bebida, e depois passar a noite numa boate.

João Eu sei! Por que não jantamos em casa, depois vamos passear na avenida até ao Tivoli, e mais tarde vamos ao T' Clube? Podemos ir ao museu no sábado. Concordas?

Maria Concordo.

João Bem, então, fica combinado.

Actividades

1 Fill in the gaps in this exercise with words from the boxes. (*Answers on page 128.*)

1. Gostaria de ir ao .... para .... um filme.

2. Vamos a um .... e .... uma bebida.

3. Preferia .... em casa.

4. Gostarias de .... ao .... amanhã?

5. Podemos .... a noite numa ....

| ver | passar | jantar | ir | tomamos | boate | cinema | museu | bar |

2 Listen to Paula and Eduardo talking about what they would like to do at the weekend, and mark their preferences on the table below. (*Answers on page 128.*)

	Eduardo		Paula	
	Sat	Sun	Sat	Sun
see a film				
eat out				
eat in				
visit a museum				
go dancing				
relax in a bar				
stroll in the centre				

3 Look at the table below of choices of activities for different days of the week, and use it to answer the questions on the tape, about what you would like to do. (*Answers on the recording and on page 128.*)

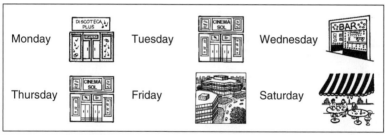

Língua

For talking about preferences, you may need the following verb forms:

Verb		I	you (fam.)	he/she/ you (pol.)	we	they/you (pl.)
gostar to like		gostaria	gostarias	gostaria	gostaríamos	gostariam
	or	gostava	gostavas	gostava	gostávamos	gostavam
preferir to prefer		prefeririia	prefeririias	prefeririia	prefeririíamos	prefeririiam
	or	preferia	preferias	preferia	preferíamos	preferiam

In each case, the second alternative is slightly more colloquial, although both are used extensively. They are equivalent to the English 'would like' and 'would prefer'.

De interesse

Some of the places mentioned in the dialogue are worth visiting if you are in Lisbon. O **Museu dos Coches** (carriage museum), full of beautiful coaches and carriages, is situated downriver, in a part of Lisbon known as **Belém** (Bethlehem). In the centre of Lisbon, you can walk down the **Avenida da Liberdade**, the main artery of the city, to the river **Tejo** (Tagus), and visit the **Tivoli** cinema halfway down.

Holidays

Discussing next year's holidays

Vocabulário

passou bem?	are you well? (colloquial)
trouxe	I have brought
vai	(you/he/she) are/is going
espero	I hope
(a) biblioteca	library
deixe-me	let me
levar	to take, carry
pintar	to paint
aprender a	to learn (how) to
cuidar de	to look after
(o) saco	(carrier) bag
(a) pintura	painting
no ano que vem	next year
no próximo ano	next year
um curso	a course
(a) cerâmica	pottery
(os) amigos	friends
a Holanda	Holland
pelo menos	at least
um mês	a month
(o) cão	dog
boa sorte!	good luck!
óptimo	great
imenso	a lot

Diálogo

Júlio Olá, Maria. Passou bem?

Maria Sim, obrigada, Júlio, mas estou um pouco cansada por causa destes livros que trouxe da biblioteca.

Júlio Deixe-me levar o seu saco, então. O que tem aqui? Livros sobre pintura; vai aprender a pintar?

Maria No ano que vem vou fazer um curso de verão sobre pintura e cerâmica.

Júlio Onde?

Maria Na Holanda. Eu e o meu marido vamos lá passar as férias. Onde vai passar as férias no próximo ano, Júlio?

Júlio Eu? Provavelmente vou visitar amigos no Brasil. Espero ficar pelo menos um mês no Rio.

Maria Óptimo! Vai gostar imenso. Mas a sua mulher vai também?

Júlio Não, ela vai ficar em casa a cuidar do cão!

Actividades

1 Translate the sentences into Portuguese using the words from the boxes.
(*Answers on page 128.*)

vou	vais	vai	vamos	vão	no ano que vem	no mês que vem

na semana que vem	ficar	ver	passear	visitar	viajar

1. We are going to visit Brazil next year.

   .... o Brasil ....

2. She is going to stay home next week.

   .... em casa ....

3. Next month you (fam.) are going to see your friends.

   .... as tuas amigas.

4. I am going to travel to Holland next year.

   .... à Holanda ....

5. Next week they are going to stroll in town.

   .... na cidade.

2 Listen to what two people are going to do during their holidays and fill in the table below with their details. (*Answers on page 128.*)

	when	what	where
1.			
2.			

3 Now take part in a dialogue about future holidays. Follow the prompts below and speak in the pauses. (*Answers on the recording and on page 128.*)

1. Next year my family and I are going to visit Denmark in the winter.
2. Where are you going to spend your holidays next month?
3. Next month I'm going to stay at home and do a Portuguese course.

Língua

To express a future action, however close or remote it may be (this afternoon, tomorrow, next year etc.), the easiest way is to simply use part of the verb 'to go' (**ir**), plus the verb representing the action to be taken. You will need to know the appropriate forms of **ir**:

eu	vou
tu	vais
ele/ela/o senhor/a senhora	vai
nós	vamos
eles/elas/os senhores/as senhoras	vão

Then you may need a few expressions of future time, such as **o ano/o mês/a semana que vem** (next year/month/week), or even **em + months/seasons**, or **as + time**. For instance:

Eu vou passar férias no Japão no ano que vem.
I'm going on holiday to Japan next year.
Tu vais viajar em Janeiro?
Are you going to travel in January?
Maria vai ver um filme às oito horas.
Maria's going to see a film at eight o'clock.

De interesse

The Portuguese love travelling and many visit the UK every year, as well as other European countries and the USA. However, they also love to return home.

The weather

Weather reports

Vocabulário

sair	to go out, leave
(a) televisão	television
(a) previsão	forecast
Portugal continental	mainland Portugal
(as) regiões	regions
(o) norte	north
(o) sul	south
(o) leste	east
(o) oeste	west
fraco	weak
moderado	moderate
parcialmente	partially
(a) temperatura	temperature
(os) graus	degrees
(o) mar	sea
(uma) ondulação	tide (height)
(a) qualidade	quality
(o) ar	air
observada	observed, noted
últimas	last, past
menos	minus

Diálogo

man Vamos ver a previsão do tempo na televisão antes de sair.

weathergirl E agora temos a previsão do tempo para hoje em todo Portugal continental: nas regiões do norte e do centro, o céu vai estar pouco nublado, com vento fraco do leste. No sul, o céu vai estar parcialmente nublado com vento moderado. As temperaturas vão chegar a quinze graus no norte, e dezassete no sul. No oeste, o mar vai ter uma ondulação de dois a três metros. A qualidade do ar observada em Lisboa nas últimas vinte e quatro horas é razoável.

man Vamos ficar em casa?

Actividades

1 Read the weather report again, and say if these statements are **verdadeiro** or **falso**. (*Answers on page 128.*)

	V	F
1. Na região do norte vai ter vento do oeste.	☐	☐
2. No sul a temperatura vai chegar a 17°.	☐	☐
3. Lisboa tem boa qualidade de ar.	☐	☐
4. O vento vai estar moderado na região central.	☐	☐
5. A ondulação do mar vai chegar a três metros no oeste.	☐	☐

2 Listen to a report on the temperatures in capital cities around the world, and complete the table below with the correct temperatures/cities. Some have already been done for you. (*Answers on page 128.*)

City	Temperature
Madrid	....
London	....
....	8°
Amsterdam	....
....	14°

3 Now it's your turn to be the weather person on TV reading a weather report. Follow the prompts below. (*Answers on the recording and on pages 128–9.*)

1. Good evening. Here we have the weather forecast for today for England.
2. In the northern region the sky will be cloudy with a moderate wind.
3. The temperatures are going to reach 18° in the south.
4. The quality of air observed in London is reasonable.

Língua

Vamos ..., as you learned in unit 33, means 'we're going to ...'. It can mean 'shall we ...?' too, eg. **vamos sair?** 'Shall we go out?'.

It is also used with other verbs in the infinitive, in the sense 'let's ...', eg. **vamos ver** 'let's see'.

De interesse

Portugal continental is mainland Portugal. Usually, on weather forecasts on TV, radio, and in the newspapers, you will also be given information on **os Açores** (the Azores Islands), and **Madeira**. These islands, out in the Atlantic, are Portuguese territories.

35 III health

Feeling ill

Vocabulário

não me sinto bem	I don't feel well
não estou nada bem	I'm not well at all
o que tem feito?	what have you been doing?
não sei	I don't know
dói-me (sing)	… hurts
doem-me (pl.)	… hurt
ter dores	to hurt (have pain)
que estranho!	how strange!
isto é grave	this is serious
cortei	I cut
magoei	I hurt
o problema	the problem
as costas	the back
as pernas	the legs
o braço	the arm
o estômago	the stomach
os dentes	the teeth
os olhos	the eyes
o dedo	the finger
o pé	the foot
caiu?	have you fallen?
hoje de manhã	this morning

 ### Diálogo

man	Não me sinto bem.
doctor	Qual é o problema?
man	Tenho dores nas costas e nas pernas.
doctor	Caiu?
man	Não. Não sei o que é. Dói-me o braço, e o estômago.
doctor	Que estranho! Isto é grave. Tem dor de cabeça?
man	Não, de cabeça não, mas doem-me os dentes e os olhos. Não estou nada bem.
doctor	Mas o que tem feito?
man	Cortei o dedo ontem, e magoei o pé hoje de manhã. Ai, que dor!
doctor	Seria melhor ir para a cama.

Actividades

1   Match the captions to the parts of the body by drawing lines.
    (*Answers on page 129.*)

   1. Dói-me o braço.
   2. Dói-me o pé.
   3. Doem-me os olhos.
   4. Dói-me o estômago.
   5. Doem-me os dentes.

2   Listen to someone talking about their ailments and mark on the table below
    what is wrong with them. (*Answers on page 129.*)

has a pain in ...				has cut ...			has hurt ...	
leg	arm	eyes	head	foot	leg	arm	leg	back

3   Take part in a dialogue yourself now. Imagine you have various ailments and
    need to tell a doctor or pharmacist about them. Follow the prompts below.
    (*Answers on the recording and on page 129.*)

   1. Hello, I don't feel very well.
   2. I have a headache and my teeth hurt.
   3. Yesterday I hurt my head and cut my finger.
   4. Not in my eyes, but my stomach aches.

Língua

Note the position of the pronouns **me/se** in the different sentences below:

dói-me	... hurts me	**não me dói**	it doesn't hurt me
sinto-me	I feel ...	**não me sinto bem**	I don't feel well
chamo-me	I am called ...	**como se chama?**	what are you called?

Usually, pronouns that are objects of a verb go after the verb, joined to it by a hyphen,
but after negatives and question words, they move before the verb.

De interesse

Before you go to Portugal, make sure you have adequate insurance to cover
medical costs (doctor, hospital, dentist). Take your completed E111 form and carry
with you all medical documentation in reference to medication you may be taking.

Time

Discussing when things happened

Vocabulário

senhor doutor	doctor (title)
começou	it started
fez	you did
comeu	you ate
fui	I went
voltei	I returned
saí	I went out
comi	I ate
cheguei	I arrived
bebi	I drank
chegámos	we arrived
almoçar	to have lunch
(a) barriga	tummy/belly
(a) ginástica	aerobics/keep-fit
(a) indigestão	indigestion
cedo	early
por volta de	around, about
logo	then
cuidado com	take care with

Diálogo

woman	Ai, senhor doutor. Não me sinto nada bem.
doctor	Qual é o problema?
woman	Dói-me muito a barriga.
doctor	Quando começou a dor?
woman	Hoje de manhã, por volta das nove horas.
doctor	O que fez ontem?
woman	Ontem, bem, de manhã fui para o trabalho cedo, voltei a casa ao meio-dia para almoçar, e saí logo para fazer ginástica.
doctor	E à noite, comeu alguma coisa?
woman	Pois sim, fui a um restaurante com uma amiga.
doctor	A que horas?
woman	Eram nove e meia quando lá chegámos. Eu comi arroz de marisco e pudim, e bebi meia garrafa de vinho. Era meia-noite quando cheguei a casa.
doctor	Acho que a senhora tem indigestão. Cuidado com a comida.

Actividades

1 Match the captions below to the pictures opposite. In each one Paulo is saying what he did yesterday. (*Answers on page 129.*)

 a) bebi vinho
 b) cheguei a casa
 c) almoçei
 d) saí para o trabalho
 e) fui ao cinema

1 2 3 4   5

2 Listen to Ana saying what time she did things yesterday. Fill in the missing details below. (*Answers on page 129.*)

    1. ....: went to work.
    2. ....: returned home for lunch.
    3. ....: went to a restaurant.
    4. ....: arrived home.

3 Now take part in a dialogue about what you did yesterday, using the prompts below to guide you. (*Answers on the recording and on page 129.*)

    1. Yesterday morning I went to work early and returned home for lunch at 1.30.
    2. Then I left to visit the library.
    3. I went to a restaurant with a friend.
    4. I ate chicken, almond cake, and I drank half a bottle of white wine.
    5. It was 11.15 when I arrived home.

Língua

Talking about things which have taken place in the past can be rather complex, so do not overconcern yourself with it at this stage. Two important things to remember:

1. In Portuguese, questions in the past do not have a word corresponding to the English 'did', as in 'what *did* you do? You simply ask 'what you did?' (**o que fez?**).
2. When talking about time in the past, use **eram** when there is more than one hour involved, and **era** for one o'clock, midday and midnight:

Eram cinco e meia.	It was 5.30.
Era uma menos dez.	It was ten to one.
Era meia-noite.	It was midnight.

De interesse

With rather late dining times, and meals and drinks which are quite hearty, indigestion is a common complaint for visitors to Portugal. The **vinho verde** ('green wine') is also more acid than normal white wines, yet most visitors want to try it as it is a Portuguese speciality.

People

Discussing jobs and professions

Vocabulário

o [que é] que faz/fazem?	what do you/they do?
professor(a)	teacher
desenhador(a)	designer
secretária	secretary
escritor(a)	writer
funcionário público	civil servant
o sobrinho, a sobrinha	the nephew, the niece
o cunhado, a cunhada	the brother-in-law, the sister-in-law
o/a primo/a	the cousin
(uma) escola	school
(uma) empresa	business
(a) informática	IT (computers)
trabalho	I work
trabalha	he/she works
trabalham	they work
o trabalho	the work
era	was
diga-me	tell me
exporta	exports
juntos	together

Diálogo

António	Diga-me uma coisa, Anne; o que é que faz?
Anne	Eu? Pois sou professora. Trabalho numa escola primária.
António	Gosta do trabalho?
Anne	Gosto sim. O meu pai também era professor, mas agora é reformado. A minha mãe é secretária.
António	E o que fazem os seus irmãos?
Anne	Bom. O meu irmão trabalha com a informática numa empresa internacional nos Estados Unidos, e a minha irmã é escritora. O meu cunhado é desenhador, portanto os dois trabalham juntos.
António	E os seus sobrinhos? Trabalham?
Anne	Não, ainda são novos. E o António? O que faz?
António	Eu trabalho com o meu primo. Temos uma pequena empresa que exporta vinhos para a Alemanha.

Actividades

1   Who does which job? Link up the Portuguese statements on the left with the correct English versions on the right. (*Answers on page 129.*)

1. Sou professora.
2. A minha prima é secretária.
3. O João trabalha com a informática.
4. O meu irmão é desenhador.

a) My cousin is a secretary.
b) My sister is a designer.
c) I am a teacher.
d) John works with computers.
e) My brother is a designer.

2 Listen to three people being interviewed about their jobs and fill in the table below with their details. Some have been done for you. (*Answers on page 129.*)

	name	profession	place of work
1.	José		
2.			
3.		civil servant	

3 Now you will play the role of Jorge Santos in a dialogue on the cassette. You may need to revise **Unit 25** for the names of relations. (*Answers on the recording and on page 129.*)

1. Good afternoon, Teresa.
2. I'm a designer. I work in an international company in Lisbon.
3. Yes, I like it a lot.
4. My wife works in a school. She's a secretary.
5. What do you do, Teresa?

Língua

You have already learned the verb **gostar** (to like). Please note that it always requires the preposition **de** when it is followed by an object or a verb.
You have probably noticed that **de** also contracts with **um/uma** and **este/esta** (this), **aquele/aquela** (that) etc.:

Gosto *do* bolo.	I like the cake.
O Manuel não gosta *duns* vinhos.	Manuel doesn't like some wines.
Gostas *desta* camisa?	Do you like this blouse?
Não gostamos *daquelas* praias.	We don't like those beaches.

NB. When asking simply 'Do you like?', **de** is not needed: **Gosta**?. The answer will then be just **gosto** (I like) or **não gosto** (I don't like).
The preposition **em** (in/on) contracts with the same words above, the 'em' becoming an 'n' which is placed at the beginning of each word, thus:
  Trabalho numa fábrica.   I work in a factory.

De interesse

As one might expect, many women in Portugal are still in what are considered 'female' occupations – teachers, secretaries, shop assistants and housewives. However, things are moving slowly, and there are some women managers, and businesswomen – although still very few in politics.

Eating out

Asking about what's on the menu

Vocabulário

já escolheram?	have you chosen yet?
vêm	they come
traga	bring
contém	contains
se quiser	if you wish
saber	to know
dá	is enough
bastante	quite, enough
feito	made
alérgico	allergic
as nossas	our
(a) porção	portion
(as) porções	portions
(o) feijão	beans
(a) cebola	onion
(as) azeitonas	olives
(o) alho	garlic
(o) pimentão	green pepper
(as) batatas fritas	chips
(a) fruta da época	fruit of the season
(o) queijo da serra	Serra cheese
um prato	a dish, plate
uma dose	a portion, helping
meia dose	half a portion, helping
uma açorda de marisco	thick bread soup with seafood
uma feijoada transmontana	bean stew from Trás-os-Montes
bacalhau na cataplana	cod cooked in a cataplana

Diálogo

waiter	Já escolheram?
customer	Sim. Queríamos uma açorda de marisco e uma feijoada transmontana. Uma coisa – meia dose dá para uma pessoa?
waiter	Dá, sim. As nossas porções são bastante grandes.
customer	Então, só meia dose da feijoada. Outra coisa, o meu marido é alérgico a cebolas, e queria saber como é feito o bacalhau na cataplana.
waiter	Bom, este prato contém bacalhau (claro!), azeitonas, tomate, alho, pimentão e cebola; mas podemos fazer sem cebola se quiser.
customer	Está bem. Os pratos vêm com salada ou legumes?
waiter	A feijoada vem com arroz, e os outros com batatas fritas e salada.
customer	Então traga uma dose de legumes também, faz favor.
waiter	Muito bem. Vão querer sobremesa?
customer	Sim. Queremos a fruta da época, e uma porção do queijo da serra. Obrigada.

Actividades

1   Fill in the gaps in this text with appropriate Portuguese words or phrases. (*Answers on page 129.*)

(We would like) .... bacalhau na cataplana, com batatas fritas e (salad) .... A minha mulher queria (a half-serving) .... da feijoada com (rice) .... (Bring) .... uma dose de legumes também, se faz favor. Para (dessert) .... queríamos (fruit) .... da época, e dois (small black coffees) ....

2   Joan is allergic to tomatoes. Listen to descriptions of what is in two dishes, ticking off the list below. You can then decide which of the two she can eat. You may need to revise **Unit 31**. (*Answers on page 129.*)

ingredients	dish 1	dish 2		dish 1	dish 2
rice	☐	☐	onion	☐	☐
garlic	☐	☐	olive	☐	☐
tomato	☐	☐	pork	☐	☐
green pepper	☐	☐	cod	☐	☐
carrot	☐	☐			

3   Now you will take part in a dialogue with a waiter about different dishes. Follow the prompts below. (*Answers on the recording and on page 129.*)

1. Yes, we would like the cataplana cod and a bean stew.   **2.** Is a half-serving enough for one person?   **3.** In that case, only a half-portion of the cod.   **4.** Do the dishes come with chips or salad?   **5.** In that case, please bring a salad as well.

Língua

Se quiser, meaning 'if you like/want', is used in many situations in everyday Portuguese. For example, if someone says to you:

Vamos ao cinema?   Shall we go to the cinema?

you could say **se quiser** (if you like/want to), or, if you are talking to more than one person, **se quiserem**.

De interesse

It is quite acceptable to order half a helping (**meia dose**) in Portugal, especially of the more filling dishes. Many menus have a separate price listed for half-helpings. A **cataplana** is a round, copper vessel of Moorish origin which works like a pressure cooker, and captures the full flavour of food cooked in it.

Accommodation

Inside a house

Vocabulário

a casa	the house
a entrada	the entrance/hall
a sala de estar	the living room
a cozinha	the kitchen
um quintal	a yard
a sala de jantar	the dining room
o jardim	the garden
a estadia	the stay
a mala	the suitcase
a porta	the door
creio	I believe
tomamos	we have/take
entre!	enter/come in!
deixe	leave
venha	come
viu	you saw
subir	to go up(stairs)
infelizmente	unfortunately
mesmo	same
separado	separate
junto com	together with
à frente	at the front
dentro	inside
aqui em cima	up here
lá em baixo	down there
em cima	upstairs
em baixo	downstairs
bem em frente	right in front

Diálogo

Sra Oliveira	Olá, e bem-vindo à nossa casa.
Charles	Obrigado. Creio que vou gostar muito da minha estadia aqui.
Sra Oliveira	Entre, faz favor. Deixe a mala aqui na entrada e venha ver a casa.
Charles	Está bem.
Sra Oliveira	Aqui à esquerda tem a sala de estar junto com uma sala de jantar. Geralmente tomamos o pequeno almoço aqui na cozinha, à sua direita. Fora da casa há um quintal.
Charles	Não tem jardim?
Sra Oliveira	Só aquele que o Charles viu à frente da casa. Vamos subir? ... Aqui em cima há três quartos – o nosso, o do nosso filho, e este, onde o Charles vai ficar. Infelizmente não tem casa de banho dentro do mesmo quarto, mas há uma em frente, aqui, nesta porta. Lá em baixo há um W.C. separado, à direita.

Actividades

1 Match the Portuguese room names to the English ones. (*Answers on page 129.*)

1. a sala de estar	**a)** the kitchen
2. o quarto	**b)** the bedroom
3. a cozinha	**c)** the dining room
4. o jardim	**d)** the garden
5. a casa de banho	**e)** the living room
6. a sala de jantar	**f)** the bathroom

2 You will hear someone describing their house as they show you around. Listen to their description and mark the names of the rooms numbered on the plans below. (*Answers on page 129.*)

em baixo

em cima

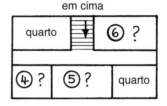

3 Using the **Língua** section below, work out the Portuguese for the following, and say your answers in the pauses on the recording. (*Answers on the recording and on page 129.*)

1. my bedrooms **2.** your (fam.) house **3.** your (polite) garden **4.** your (polite) kitchens **5.** his living-room **6.** her dining room

Língua

So far you have come across isolated examples of the words for 'my', 'his', 'your' etc. Here is a simplified table of all the forms you may have encountered so far:

	singular		plural	
	masculine	*feminine*	*masculine*	*feminine*
my	**o meu**	**a minha**	**os meus**	**as minhas**
your (fam.)	**o teu**	**a tua**	**os teus**	**as tuas**
your (pol.)	**o seu**	**a sua**	**os seus**	**as suas**
our	**o nosso**	**a nossa**	**os nossos**	**as nossas**
his	**o ... dele**	**a ... dele**	**os ... dele**	**as ... dele**
her	**o ... dela**	**a ... dela**	**os ... dela**	**as ... dela**
their	**o ... deles/as**	**a ... deles/as**	**os ... deles/as**	**as ... deles/as**

Remember that the word you choose from the table depends on whether the possessed article is masculine or feminine, and singular or plural, eg.

my daughter	**a minha filha**	my son	**o meu filho**
your children	**os seus filhos**	your sisters	**as suas irmãs**

De interesse

Casa in Portuguese means both house and home (or **lar**). Many Portuguese people refer to their **casa**, although it is more likely to be an apartment, either in an old city-centre traditional building, or in a modern block on the outskirts.

Travel

A visit to a petrol station

Vocabulário

encha	fill
verificar	to check
vendemos	we sell
vai ter de	you're going to have to
fica a ...	is at a distance of ...
uns ... quilómetros	some ... kilometres
uma estação de serviço	a service station
um posto de gasolina	a petrol station
uma bomba de gasolina	a petrol pump
uma oficina de automóveis	a garage
(o) depósito	tank
(a) pressão	air pressure
(os) pneus	tyres
(o) gasóleo	diesel
(a) gasolina	petrol
super	4-star
normal	2-star
sem chumbo	unleaded
um litro	a litre
litro e meio	one and a half litres
um mapa	a map
pronto	right then, ready
adeus	goodbye

Diálogo

driver	Olá, bom dia. Encha o depósito, por favor.
attendant	Quer super ou normal?
driver	Super, se faz favor, mas tem gasolina sem chumbo?
attendant	Temos sim, senhora.
driver	Então, queria sem chumbo.
attendant	Pronto. São dois mil e quatrocentos escudos.
driver	Tem óleo?
attendant	Temos. O que quer? Um litro? Litro e meio? ...
driver	Pode ser um litro. E tem mapas da região?
attendant	Não vendemos mapas. A senhora vai ter de comprar um na cidade mais próxima.
driver	É longe daqui?
attendant	Fica a uns dez quilómetros daqui.
driver	Obrigada. Vou verificar a água e a pressão dos pneus também.

Actividades

1 Match the Portuguese and English sentences. (*Answers on page 129.*)

1. dois litros de óleo
2. dois mil e quatrocentos escudos
3. dez litros de gasolina super
4. cinco litros de gasóleo
5. mil duzentos e cinquenta escudos

a) five litres of diesel
b) two litres of four-star petrol
c) 1,250 escudos
d) ten litres of four-star petrol
e) two litres of oil
f) 2,400 escudos
g) five litres of two-star petrol

2 Listen to two people being served at a petrol station and mark on the table what they require, and how much. (*Answers on page 129.*)

	quantity of petrol					quantity of oil
	2-star	4-star	leaded	unleaded	diesel	
1.						
2.						

3 Take part in a conversation at a petrol station, following the prompts below. (*Answers on the recording and on page 129.*)

1. Good morning. Please fill up the tank.
2. 2-star unleaded, please.
3. Do you have oil?
4. 2 litres.
5. Do you sell maps of the region?
6. OK. How much is that?
7. Thank you. Goodbye.

Língua

To say 'nearest', 'furthest', 'fastest', 'cheapest', etc., you use **mais** (more) and the relevant adjective (**próximo**, **longe**, **rápido**, **barato** respectively):

mais próximo	nearest	**mais longe**	furthest
mais rápido	fastest	**mais barato**	cheapest

If you are describing an object, such as 'the fastest train', the word order is: **o comboio mais rápido**. Remember also to make the adjectives agree in gender (masculine/feminine) and number (singular/plural):

a camisa mais barata	the cheapest blouse
as praias mais próximas	the nearest beaches

De interesse

Um posto de gasolina (a petrol station) will usually only serve petrol requirements, and not many are open 24 hours. On country roads you may only come across **uma bomba de gasolina** (a single petrol pump), which is open for even fewer hours. If you need help with your vehicle on the road, you will need to find **uma estação de serviço** (a service station), or, in the towns, **uma oficina de automóveis** (a car-repair garage).

UNIT 45 | Directions
Travelling by car

Vocabulário

dizer	to say
diz	says
é só	you only have to, it's just …
a estrada	the road
o caminho	the way
o sinal	the sign
os semáforos	the traffic lights
uma rotunda	a roundabout
(os) sinais de trânsito	road signs
(a) passagem de peões	pedestrian crossing
(o) perigo	danger
a ajuda	the help
(a) portagem	toll
voltar para trás	to turn back
seguir	to follow
chegará	you will arrive
parece	it seems
complicado	complicated
devagar	slow(ly)
pare	stop
sem saida	no exit

Diálogo

visitor O senhor desculpe, pode me dizer se este é o caminho para Loulé?

man Para Loulé? Não é por aqui. A senhora tem que voltar para trás até aos semáforos. Depois, precisa de virar à direita e tomar a estrada para Vila Real. Logo vai ver uma rotunda – é só seguir o sinal que diz Loulé, e pronto, chegará.

visitor Parece um pouco complicado. É longe?

man Não é muito longe. Loulé fica a uns trinta e cinco quilómetros daqui.

visitor Está bem. Obrigada pela ajuda.

Actividades

1 Match the road signs to the captions. (*Answers on page 129.*)

1. 2. 3. 4. 5.

a) Passagem de peões **b)** Semáforos **c)** Siga em frente **d)** Proibido virar à direita **e)** Cuidado–animais

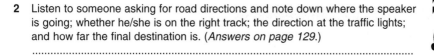
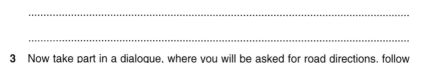

2   Listen to someone asking for road directions and note down where the speaker is going; whether he/she is on the right track; the direction at the traffic lights; and how far the final destination is. (*Answers on page 129.*)

....

....

....

3   Now take part in a dialogue, where you will be asked for road directions. follow the prompts below. (*Answers on the recording and on page 129.*)

   1. For Viseu? No, it's not through here.
   2. Turn back to the traffic lights, then turn left and take the road for Guarda.
   3. Next you will see a roundabout – just follow the sign for Viseu, and there you are, you'll arrive.
   4. Yes, it is a bit far. Viseu is some 95 Km from here.

Língua

There are two ways of saying 'for' in Portuguese: **por** and **para**:

por	para
through/by/along	direction to/towards

As you saw in Unit 17, remember that **por** becomes **pelo, pela, pelos, pelas** when contracted with the words for 'the'.

O caminho *para* Loulé	the way to Loulé
Vamos passar *pelo* parque	let's go through the park.

You will also come across further usages of **por** and **para** as you learn more Portuguese.

De interesse

Driving in Portugal can be very hit and miss (sometimes, unfortunately, quite literally!). Roads are often in a bad state of repair, drivers seem oblivious to the laws and etiquette of driving, and some stretches of road are notoriously dangerous, such as the coastal stretch between Lisbon and Estoril, known as **A Marginal**, which is considered one of the most dangerous in Europe. Some of the road signs you may need to look out for are shown on the opposite page.

 **Town amenities**

Sports and leisure facilities

Vocabulário

os desportos	the sports
uma piscina	a swimming pool
um clube	a sports club
(o) ténis	tennis
(o) futebol	football
um parque	a park
um campo de golfe	a golf course
um centro hípico	a horse riding centre
o lago	the lake
um passeio	a walk/ride
de barquinho	by (small) boat
(o) centro de lazer	leisure centre
(o) sócio	member
(os) adultos	adults
(as) crianças	children
municipal	municipal/public
além de	as well as/besides
além disto	as well as this
fazer piquenique	to have a picnic
correr	to run
jogar	to play
andar a cavalo	to ride a horse

 ### Diálogo

Ao turismo

woman	Bom dia. Diga, se faz favor.
visitor	Bom dia. Queria saber se tem informações sobre os desportos na cidade.
woman	Claro. Nesta cidade temos uma boa piscina municipal, que abre todos os dias menos segunda. Também há um clube de futebol e outro de ténis.
visitor	E para a família?
woman	Bom, além da piscina, há dois parques onde uma família pode fazer piquenique, correr, e fazer um passeio de barquinho no lago.
visitor	Há um campo de golfe?
woman	Aqui não há, mas há um bom clube na cidade mais próxima, só que tem que ser sócio para jogar. Além disto, há um centro hípico onde pode andar a cavalo, na estrada de Lagoa.

Actividades

1 Fill in the gaps in the text with words from the boxes. (*Answers on page 129.*)

Aqui pode fazer muitos .... Na cidade há uma .... e um centro .... onde pode andar a .... Também há um bom .... de golfe e um clube de .... mas tem que ser .... para .... Uma família pode fazer .... no ....

hípico	ténis	piquenique	piscina	campo	jogar	desportos	cavalo	sócio	parque

2 Listen to someone enquiring about leisure facilities and tick what is available. (*Answers on page 129.*)

horse-riding ☐
park ☐
golf course ☐
football ☐
tennis club ☐
picnic areas ☐
swimming ☐
boating lake ☐

3 Imagine you want to find out about certain leisure facilities and go to the **turismo** to ask about availability and opening times. (*Answers on the recording and on page 129.*)

1. Good morning. Do you have any information on the sports in the city?
2. Does the swimming pool open every day?
3. Do you have to be a member to play golf?
4. Where is the golf course?
5. Thank you.

Língua

The Portuguese like to add **-inho/a** to the end of words. This has the effect of not only making an object seem smaller, eg. **um barco** (boat) **barquinho** (little boat), but can also make words and phrases sound more friendly, cuter and more expressive:

obrigado/a	thank you	**obrigadinho/a**	thanks
um pouco	a little	**um pouquinho**	a tiny bit
um prato	a plate/dish	**um pratinho**	small plate/'nibbles'

De interesse

Portugal does not have an extensive system of **centros de lazer** (leisure centres), even in the larger cities. Most places at least have **uma piscina municipal** (public baths), and **quadras de ténis** (tennis courts). Many people actually play tennis and football on the dusty grounds of the local high schools.

The town centre

Shopping for souvenirs

Vocabulário

à procura de	looking for
recomenda	(you) recommend
compra	you buy
embrulhar	to wrap up
por exemplo	for example
à mão	by hand
tudo	everything
uma lembrança	a souvenir
(as) toalhas de mesa	tablecloths
(os) azulejos	ornamental tiles
(os) painéis	tile panels
um galo de Barcelos	Barcelos cockerel
(o) símbolo	symbol
um xaile	a shawl
(os) brincos	earrings
(o) artesanato	crafts
a fábrica	the factory
típica	typical
(a) filigrana	filigree
bordadas	embroidered
pesado	heavy
nacional	national
preto	black
vermelho	red
as cores	the colours

Diálogo

customer Bom dia, minha senhora. Estou à procura duma lembrança típica de Portugal para a minha mulher. O que recomenda?

assistant Tenho umas coisas muito lindas para senhoras. Por exemplo, há estas toalhas de mesa brancas, bordadas à mão. Também há em vermelho.

customer Tem azulejos?

assistant Tenho sim. Aqui estão. Há desde estes pequenos até estes grandes painéis.

customer Não quero nada muito pesado.

assistant Então, por que não compra um galo de Barcelos, que é o nosso símbolo nacional? As cores são bonitas – laranja, vermelho, azul e preto.

customer Boa ideia. Também vou levar este xaile e estes brincos de filigrana. Pode-me embrulhar tudo?

assistant Claro.

Actividades

1 Put the correct form of the adjective in these sentences. Remember to check if the objects are masculine, or feminine, and singular or plural. (*Answers on page 129.*)

1. Quero um xaile .... (preto), por favor.
2. Temos estas toalhas de mesa .... (vermelho)
3. Vou levar estes brincos .... (lindo)
4. Os painéis são muito .... (pesado)
5. Por que não leva um galo .... (nacional)

2   Listen to a conversation in a gift shop, and mark on the table what there is to buy. (*Answers on page 129.*)

gift	yes	no	red	white	black	orange	blue	no specific colour
Barcelos cockerel								
tablecloths								
tiles								
tile panels								
shawl								

3   Now take part in a dialogue in a gift shop, where you are looking for souvenirs. (*Answers on the recording and on page 129.*)

1. Good morning. I'm looking for a typical souvenir of Portugal for my daughter. What do you recommend?
2. Do you have any black shawls?
3. Do you have any tiles?
4. I don't want anything very heavy.
5. Good idea, and I'll also take a black shawl.

Língua

Tudo is a neutral word which means 'everything', ie. nothing is specified. It never changes form, unlike the adjective **todo (toda, todos, todas)**, meaning 'all the', 'every', which agrees with the words it is describing:

todos os dias	every day
toda a maçã	all the apple
but **quero tudo**	I want everything

De interesse

Lembranças (souvenirs) are varied in Portugal. **Artesanato** (crafts) are widespread, and in country areas you can often see people creating their products – weaving, making pottery, lace, etc. Earthenware pottery (**cerâmica**) is popular in the North, and cheaper in the smaller towns. Lace (**renda**) often comes in from Madeira and is a little more pricey, but exquisite and well worth the price. Tiles (**azulejos**) are available everywhere – you can buy number tiles for your house at a very low price, up to full size picture panels, which are much more expensive. In Lisbon search out the factory which makes them – the **Fábrica de Sant'ana**.

Personal choices

Talking about sports and hobbies

Vocabulário

(o) tempo livre	free time
(o) tempo de lazer	leisure time
(a) música	music
(os) jornais	newspapers
(os) romances policiais	police novels
a óleo	in oils
praticar (desportos)	to play (sports)
faz bem	is good/does good
faz mal	is bad/does bad
detesto	I detest
odeia	hates(s)
prefere	prefer(s)
preferido	favourite
nadar	to swim
ouvir	to hear, listen
ler	to read
fumar	to smoke
mesmo	even
andar de bicicleta	to go bike riding
a mente	the mind

Diálogo

Pedro   O que é que tu gostas de fazer no tempo livre?

Ana   Gosto muito de praticar desportos sempre que posso.

Pedro   E qual é o teu desporto preferido?

Ana   Adoro nadar, e também jogar golfe.

Pedro   Não gostas de fazer coisas em casa?

Ana   Em geral detesto ficar em casa, mas de vez em quando gosto de pintar a óleo. E tu, Pedro, o que é que fazes no teu tempo de lazer?

Pedro   Eu prefiro ficar em casa a ouvir música e a ler. Adoro passar umas horas a ler jornais e romances policiais. A minha mulher odeia ficar dentro de casa – ela prefere andar de bicicleta, mesmo no inverno!

Ana   Faz bem à saúde.

Pedro   Sim, mas o ler faz bem à mente!

Actividades

1   The verbs underlined are all in the wrong position! Put them in the correct sentence and give real meaning to the text. (*Answers on pages 129–30.*)

Gosto muito de ir à piscina para <u>andar</u>. A minha filha prefere <u>pintar</u> jornais em casa, e o meu filho adora <u>ouvir música</u> a óleo. Pessoalmente, detesto <u>nadar</u> de bicicleta, mas gosto de <u>ler</u> jazz.

2 Listen to the following survey about what two people do in their free time and note down in the space provided what each person does/ doesn't like doing. (*Answers on page 130.*)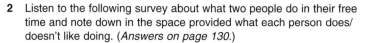

Speaker **1** likes ....

does not like ....

Speaker **2** likes ....

does not like ....

3 Imagine you are Sra Silva and you are being asked about your hobbies. Follow the prompts below. (*Answers on the recording and on page 130.*)

1. I like riding a bike and swimming.
2. The bike.
3. I sometimes like listening to music.
4. My husband likes reading. He hates sports.

Língua

In English we often use verbs as nouns (verbal nouns), as in reading, smoking, walking, etc. In Portuguese you can convey these forms by using the structure **o + verb in the infinitive** (its normal form):

O ler faz bem à mente.	Reading is good for the mind.
O fumar faz mal.	Smoking does harm.
O andar é bom.	Walking is good.

De interesse

The Portuguese are very keen on music, from country-style folk groups (**ranchos folclóricos**) who sing and dance, to the national **fado**, which can either be sombre and nostalgic, or livelier and evocative. They also like opera, jazz, classical and modern rock. The Portuguese guitar, heard in **fado**, is unlike the Spanish: it is pear-shaped, has double metal strings, and is a surviving relation of the zither.

Holidays

Discussing last year's holidays

Vocabulário

passou	you spent
passei	I spent
foi	it was
fomos	we went
gostaram	you liked
gostámos	we liked
gostei	I liked
perdemos	we lost
vimos	we saw
adorámos	we loved
visitámos	we visited
visitei	I visited
uma experiência	an experience
(a) viagem	journey
(a) emoção	excitement
positiva	positive
cansativo	tiring
cheios de	full of
(o) México	Mexico
o ano passado	last year

Diálogo

Júlia Onde passou as últimas férias?

João O ano passado eu e a minha mulher fomos para os Estados Unidos.

Júlia E gostaram?

João Gostámos, mas perdemos uma mala e eu não gostei muito da comida.

Júlia Mas foi uma experiência positiva?

João Foi, sim. Vimos muitas coisas novas, visitámos muitas cidades e praias e fomos até ao México.

Júlia Foi cansativo?

João Um pouco, sim, mas adorámos a viagem, e chegámos ao hotel cheios de emoção.

Actividades

1 Choose the correct verb to fill in the blanks in these sentences.
(*Answers on page 130.*)

a) bebemos   **b)** perdemos   **c)** visitámos   **d)** vimos   **e)** chegámos
f) adorámos

1. A semana passada .... Londres.
2. .... a comida.
3. .... muito vinho.
4. Nas férias .... muitas coisas novas.
5. .... às dez horas.
6. Infelizmente, ... as nossas malas.

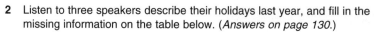
2 Listen to three speakers describe their holidays last year, and fill in the missing information on the table below. (*Answers on page 130.*)

	went to	with whom	liked	didn't like	visited
1.					
2.					
3.					

3 Take part in a conversation about holidays, using the prompts below to guide you. (*Answers on the recording and on page 130.*)

1. Last year, I went to Madeira with my family.
2. We liked it a lot but my wife did not like the food.
3. Yes, we visited Funchal and saw the *levadas*.
4. Yes, but also a little tiring.

Língua

In Unit 36 you were introduced to the past tense of some verbs. Here is a table of some other verbs in the past tense you may want to use at this stage.

		eu	*tu*	*ele/ela* *o senhor/* *a senhora*	*nós*	*eles/elas* *os senhores/* *as senhoras*
beber	drink	**bebi**	**bebeste**	**bebeu**	**bebemos**	**beberam**
comer	eat	**comi**	**comeste**	**comeu**	**comemos**	**comeram**
chegar	arrive	**cheguei**	**chegaste**	**chegou**	**chegámos**	**chegaram**
gostar	like	**gostei**	**gostaste**	**gostou**	**gostámos**	**gostaram**
visitar	visit	**visitei**	**visitaste**	**visitou**	**visitámos**	**visitaram**
ver	see	**vi**	**viste**	**viu**	**vimos**	**viram**
ir	go	**fui**	**foste**	**foi**	**fomos**	**foram**

This past tense in Portuguese translates both as 'I have done' and 'I did'.

Comi muito.	I have eaten a lot/I ate a lot.
Ela visitou a França.	She has visited France/She visited France.

De interesse

There are almost half a million Portuguese people currently living in the USA, many working in the hotel and catering industry.

46 The weather

Talking about climates

Vocabulário

mais ou menos	more or less
tão bom	so good
demasiado	too (much)
variável	changeable
parecido	alike
igual	the same
seco	dry
tropical	tropical
perfeito	perfect
refrescante	refreshing
chove	it rains
não sabia	I didn't know
não aguento	I can't stand, I hate
não aguento … nem …	I can't stand … or …
(a) Grã-Bretanha	Great Britain

Diálogo

Charles	Eu gosto imenso de Portugal porque o clima é tão bom.
Alexandra	Nem sempre, Charles. No inverno o clima cá é bastante variável. No sul é quente, e, às vezes, também chove; no centro e no norte é frio.
Charles	Ah, sim? Eu não sabia. Então, o clima do inverno é parecido com o nosso, na Grã-Bretanha. Mas o clima da primavera e do verão é melhor, não é?
Alexandra	Sim, é. O nosso clima de verão em geral é quente e seco; do norte ao sul, e do oeste ao leste, é mais ou menos igual.
Charles	Não aguento um clima demasiado frio, nem tropical. Portanto, Portugal é perfeito para mim.

Actividades

1   Look at the dialogue again, then say whether these statements are **verdadeiro** or **falso**. (*Answers on page 130.*)

V F

1. No inverno, o clima em Portugal é variável.

2. No sul, é muito frio no inverno.

3. O clima em Portugal no inverno é diferente do clima da Grã-Bretanha.

4. O clima de verão em Portugal não é muito quente.

5. O Charles não gosta de clima frio.

2 Listen to a description of the varying climate in different parts of Brazil, and mark on the table opposite the details you are given. (*Answers on page 130.*)

	north	south	east	west
winter				
summer				

3 Now take part in a dialogue about the climate in Great Britain. Follow the prompts below. (*Answers on the recording and on page 130.*)

1. Not always, Maria. Our climate here is quite variable.
2. In the winter it is cold in the north and it rains a lot.
3. In the summer it is hot in the south and quite hot in the north.
4. It is a little, but the climate in Portugal in the spring and summer is better.
5. I don't like too hot a climate, so the climate in Great Britain is perfect for me.

Língua

Don't forget that when talking about climates you will use the verb **ser** the 'permanent' verb 'to be', because climates are seen to be unchanging. However, if you are talking about the weather on a particular day you should use **estar**:

O clima em Portugal é muito bom.	The climate in Portugal is very good.
O tempo hoje não está bom.	The weather today isn't good.

De interesse

Current climatic changes around the globe have also affected parts of Portugal. Long, dry periods and, at the other extreme, heavy rainfalls, both continue to bring chaos to the country at different times in the year.

47 Ill health

A trip to the hospital

Vocabulário

o médico	the doctor
um momentinho	just a short time, (for) just a moment
uma radiografia	an x-ray
um gesso	a plaster cast
o pulso	the wrist
o tornozelo	the ankle
o joelho	the knee
o chapéu	the hat
inchado	swollen
torcido	twisted, sprained
partido	broken
lavar	to wash
sentar-se	to sit down
tentei	I tried
tirar	to take
mandar	to send
atravessar	to cross
(fui) atropelado/a	(I was) knocked down
penso que	I think (that)
o que aconteceu?	what happened

Diálogo

woman	Faz favor, preciso de ver um médico.
receptionist	Qual é o problema?
woman	Penso que tenho o pulso partido, e doem-me o tornozelo e o joelho.
receptionist	Um momento, sim? Quer sentar-se um momentinho?
doctor	O que aconteceu?
woman	Tentei atravessar a avenida hoje de manhã, e fui atropelada por uma bicicleta.
doctor	Vou mandar a senhora tirar uma radiografia. O pulso está partido. Vai ter que ficar quatro semanas em gesso. Também a senhora tem um tornozelo torcido, e o joelho está inchado. Vai ter que descansar muito.

Actividades

1 Fill in the gaps in these sentences with words from the boxes opposite. Use each box once. (*Answers on page 130.*)

  1. Vou ter que ficar três semanas com um gesso porque tenho ....
  2. Faz favor, preciso de ver ....
  3. O joelho está partido, então vai ter que ficar em ....
  4. A senhora precisa de tirar .... porque tem um pulso partido.
  5. Vai ter que descansar a mão muito porque tem ....

| um | uma | um | uma | um | inchado | partido | médico |

| tornozelo | gesso | pulso | radiografia |

2 Listen to two patients being told what is wrong with them, and what the remedy is, and mark on the table below. You may need to revise **Unit 35** for parts of the body. (*Answers on page 130.*)

	affected limb	problem	plaster cast?	how long?	rest?	how long?
1.						
2.						

3 Now imagine you have had an accident and you need to visit the hospital. Start the dialogue with the first prompt below. (*Answers on the recording and on page 130.*)

1. I need to see a doctor, please.
2. I think I have a broken ankle.
3. This morning a bicycle knocked me down.
4. Am I going to have to rest?

Língua

When talking about parts of the body, you do not need to use the words for 'my', 'your', etc. You simply refer to the limb:

Tenho o pulso partido.   My wrist is broken. (lit. 'I have the wrist broken.')
Vai lavar as mãos.   Go and wash your hands.

This also applies to clothing:

Vou pôr o chapéu.   I'm going to put my hat on. (lit. 'I'm going to put on the hat.')

In Portuguese, certain verbs, like the verb 'to sit down', **sentar-se**, are followed by a pronoun (**se**) which means 'self' ('sit oneself down'). These are called 'reflexive verbs', and they are used with these 'reflexive pronouns':

I	*you (fam.)*	*he/she/it/you (form.)*	*we*	*they/you (pl.)*
-me	**-te**	**-se**	**-nos**	**-se**

In English, the word 'self' is not always present (as in 'sit down'). As with other pronouns, the reflexive goes before the verb in negatives and questions, otherwise its normal place is after.

De interesse

Unfortunately, the Health Service in Portugal still lacks efficiency, so you may face long waits at hospitals and health centres. There will also be a lot of form-filling – make sure you have relevant insurance details on you.

Time

Asking the time

Vocabulário

que horas são?	What time is it?
são ...	it is ... (lit. 'they are')
a tempo	in time
faltam ... minutos	there are ... minutes (before)
começar	to begin
começa	begins
acabas de	you have just ...
perguntar	to ask (a question)
apressar-se	to hurry
achar	to find
estacionar	to park
estamos	we are
divertir-nos	to enjoy ourselves
à hora	on time
mesmo à hora	right on time
o carro	the car
a peça	the play
calma!	calm down!

Diálogo

Carlos	Que horas são, Paula?
Paula	São sete e um quarto.
Carlos	Bom, ainda chegamos a tempo.
Paula	A que horas começa a peça?
Carlos	Às oito. Que horas são agora?
Paula	Acabas de perguntar – agora são sete e vinte.
Carlos	Faltam quarenta minutos para começar a peça, e ainda temos que achar um lugar onde estacionar o carro, comprar os bilhetes, e sentar-nos. Temos que nos apressar. Que horas são, Paula?
Paula	São oito menos dez. Calma, Carlos. Aqui estamos. Chegámos mesmo à hora. Vamos divertir-nos.

Actividades

1 Match each of these five clocks with the correct time phrase. (*Answers on page 130*.)

Que horas são?

 1.   2.   3.   4.   5.

_____ _____ _____ _____ _____

a) cinco e meia **b)** sete horas **c)** dez menos um quarto **d)** nove e vinte
e) quatro menos dez **f)** nove menos quarenta e cinco **g)** seis horas

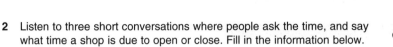
2 Listen to three short conversations where people ask the time, and say what time a shop is due to open or close. Fill in the information below. (*Answers on page 130.*)

	what time is it?	going where?	open at?	closed at?
1.				
2.				
3.				

3 Imagine you are trying to get to the bank on time. Take part in a dialogue like the one on the opposite page. (*Answers on the recording and on page 130.*)

1. Sandra, what time is it?
2. Good, there's still time to get there.
3. At three.
4. Yes, but we still have to find a place to park the car.
5. We're right on time. Let's go in.

Língua

Asking and giving the time is very similar to what you learned in Unit 24. The question **Que horas são?**, will be answered with **São** …, except when it is one o'clock, midday and midnight, when the time will be preceded by **é** …, eg. **é meia-noite** ('it is midnight'). You can also ask someone the time by saying **Tem as horas?**, and say **faltam dez minutos para as oito horas** instead of **são oito menos dez**.

De interesse

The Portuguese are not usually exacting when it comes to time-keeping. Don't be surprised to be kept waiting if you arrange to meet people, and, if you are invited to a Portuguese home for a social event, it's quite acceptable to arrive 10 to 15 minutes late.

A que horas começa o filme?

People

Talking about age

Diálogo

António	Anne, venha conhecer os meus netos. Este é o meu neto Mário, e esta é a minha neta Luísa.
Anne	Muito prazer. Quantos anos têm?
António	O Mário, que é o mais velho, tem dez anos, e a Luísa, que é mais nova, tem oito.
Anne	Eles são muito bonitos.
António	Ainda tem os avós, Anne?
Anne	Tenho duas avós, e um avô, mas o outro faleceu. Mas tenho muitos tios. A minha tia Mary fez setenta anos a semana passada.
António	E quando é o seu dia de anos, Anne?
Anne	Faço anos no dia quinze de Setembro.

Actividades

1   Match up the descriptions to the birthday cards below. (*Answers on page 130.*)

1. A avó de Sônia fez sessenta e cinco anos.   **a)**

2. O avô de Roberto fez oitenta anos.   **b)**

3. O Fernando tem vinte e um anos.   **c)**

4. A minha neta Alice vai fazer quinze anos.   **d)**

5. A Marli fez dezoito anos.   **e)**

2 Listen to three people from José's family saying what their relation to him is and what their ages are. Fill in their details on the table. (*Answers on page 130.*)

	relation to José	age
1.		
2.		
3.		

3 Now take part in a conversation about family members and their ages. Follow the prompts below. (*Answers on the recording and on page 130.*)

1. Paulo, come and meet my children.
2. David, who is the oldest, is 16 and Laura, who is younger, is 14.
3. David's birthday is on the 25th of March and Laura had her birthday last week.
4. My birthday is on the 3rd of November.

Língua

When talking about ages, you use the verb 'to have' (**ter**), plus the number of years (**anos**) someone has. You will need to know the relevant forms of the verb:

eu	tu	ele/ela	nós	eles/elas
tenho	**tens**	**tem**	**temos**	**têm**

'To have a birthday' is **fazer anos** (lit. 'to make years'), so you may need forms of the verb **fazer**:

eu	tu	ele/ela	nós	eles/elas
faço	**fazes**	**faz**	**fazemos**	**fazem**

Note how the date is done: **no dia dez de Junho** (on the 10th of June).
Note also how to make comparisons:

mais velho/a	older	**o/a mais velho/a**	the oldest
mais novo/a	younger	**o/a mais novo/a**	the youngest

De interesse

The Portuguese enjoy birthday parties, and big family gatherings often take place when an older member of the family is celebrating. A huge spread is usually laid on, with lots of extremely tempting sweets!

UNIT 50 Eating out

Making a complaint

Vocabulário

falta/m	is/are missing, lacking
trazer	to bring
acontecem	(they) happen
não pedimos	we did not order
mandámos	we sent
de volta	back
enfim	after all
peço desculpa	I'm sorry
pela demora	for the delay
a demora	the delay
um garfo	a fork
uma faca	a knife
uma colher	a spoon
umas coisinhas	some little things
a cerveja	the beer
a conta	the bill
o peru	the turkey
o copo	the glass
sujo	dirty
movimentado	busy
morno	warm
errado	wrong
rachado	chipped

Diálogo

customer	Faz favor!
waiter	Diga, faz favor.
customer	Faltam dois garfos e uma faca aqui, e esta colher está suja. Pode trazer outros?
waiter	Com certeza. Um momento só.
waiter	Pronto, aqui estão. Peço desculpa pela demora – hoje está muito movimentado, e, enfim, estas coisas acontecem.
customer	Só mais umas coisinhas – o bacalhau está frio, a cerveja está morna, o copo está rachado e a salada não está boa.
customer	Faz favor. Acho que a conta está errada. Nós não pedimos o peru, e mandámos a salada de volta.
waiter	Vou verificar.

Actividades

1 Match up the Portuguese and English expressions. (*Answers on page 130.*)

1. A colher está suja.
2. O copo está rachado.
3. Falta uma faca.
4. A conta está errada.
5. O peru está frio.

a) There's a knife missing.
b) The spoon is dirty.
c) There's a fork missing.
d) The bill is wrong.
e) The glass is chipped.
f) The cup is dirty.
g) The turkey is cold.

2 Listen to three people making complaints, and mark on the table what the problem is. (*Answers on page 130.*)

	item	problem
1.		
2.		
3.		

3 Imagine you are eating out and you have some problems you need to complain about. Let the prompts guide you through a conversation with the waiter. (*Answers on the recording and on page 130.*)

1. Excuse me!
2. There are two knives missing and this fork is dirty. Can you bring some others?
3. Another thing, the turkey isn't good, and this glass is chipped.
4. I think the bill is wrong. We sent the turkey back.
5. Thanks.

Língua

To say something is missing, or lacking, use **falta** for one item and **faltam** for more than one. You can use these verbs as follows:

Falta dinheiro.	There's no money.
Falta tempo.	There's not enough time.
Faltam dez minutos para as três.	It's ten to three.

De interesse

The Portuguese word for turkey has an interesting historical origin. When Spanish and Portuguese explorers arrived in Peru, they found a strange bird which was a local delicacy, and highly venerated. It was brought back to the Iberian peninsula and in Portugal was named after the land from whence it came – o peru.

Accommodation

When things don't work

Vocabulário

não funciona	doesn't work
pingar	to drip
dar uma olhadela	to have a look
descongelar	to defrost
em primeiro lugar	firstly
por conseguinte	consequently
totalmente	totally
inteiro	entire, whole
a noite inteira	the whole night
alguém	somebody
ninguém	nobody
quais são ...?	what are ...?
o apartamento	the apartment
o chuveiro	the shower
o frigorífico	the fridge
a torneira	the tap
o lavatório	the washbasin
o ar condicionado	the air-conditioning
abafado	stuffy

Diálogo

guest	Estamos no apartamento vinte e três, e temos alguns problemas.
receptionist	Quais são os problemas?
guest	Bom, em primeiro lugar, o chuveiro não funciona – não há água quente. Também a torneira no lavatório não fecha totalmente, e a água está a pingar a noite inteira.
receptionist	Vou ver se alguém pode ir dar uma olhadela para os senhores.
guest	Há outra coisa, parece que o ar condicionado não funciona bem, e por conseguinte está muito abafado dentro do quarto. O frigorífico não está muito frio, e a comida começou a descongelar.
receptionist	Vou ver se há outro apartamento.
guest	Boa ideia!

Actividades

1 Fill in the gaps in these sentences with suitable words from the boxes.
(*Answers on page 130.*)

1. O .... não está frio.
2. O ar .... não funciona bem.
3. Não há .... quente.
4. A torneira não .... totalmente.
5. O .... não funciona.
6. A .... está a descongelar.

água	comida	fecha	frigorífico	chuveiro	condicionado

2 Listen to two people making complaints about their apartments, and tick on the list below which problems each one has. (*Answers on page 130.*)

	1	2
shower not working		
tap won't turn off		
air-conditioning not working		
fridge not working		

3 Using the **Língua** section below as a guide, answer the questions on the recording negatively. (*Answers on the recording and on page 130.*)

eg. **Tem alguma laranja?**   Do you have an orange?
Não tenho nenhuma.   No, I don't have one.

Remember to use the correct form of the verb **ter** in each case.

Língua

Ways of expressing 'some' and 'none':

masculine singular	feminine singular	masculine plural	feminine plural
algum/um	**alguma/uma**	**alguns/uns**	**algumas/umas**
a	a	some	some
nenhum	**nenhuma**	**nenhuns**	**nenhumas**
a/one	a/one	none	none

alguém (somebody) and **ninguém** (nobody) never change form.

Maria tem algumas blusas.	Maria has some blouses.
Não tenho nenhum jornal.	I don't have a/any newspaper.
Alguém tem dinheiro?	Does anyone have (any) money?

De interesse

Problems with water and drainage are probably the most common for holiday-makers in Portugal. In the Algarve, there may be water restrictions from time to time. The drainage system is poor in many places, and you are often requested not to flush paper down the toilet!

Travel

Air travel

Vocabulário

(a) saída	exit/departure
(a) chegada	arrival
o aeroporto	the airport
o/a passageiro/a	the passenger
o/a controlador/a de bagagem	the luggage check-in attendant
um atraso	a delay
a balança	the weighing scales
o saco	the bag, carrier
o vôo	the flight
a alfândega	the customs
o oficial da alfândega	the customs official
a porta	the gate (door)
nada	nothing
a declarar	to declare

Diálogos

Departing ...

attendant	O senhor tem passaporte e bilhete?
passenger	Sim, aqui.
attendant	Quer fumador, ou não fumador?
passenger	Não fumador, por favor.
attendant	Quer passar a sua mala à balança, se faz favor? Só tem esta?
passenger	Só, e este saco que vou levar comigo.
attendant	Está bem. O vôo BA123 para Londres vai ter um atraso de uma hora. Pode passar para a porta número dezoito.

Arriving ...

customs official	Tem alguma coisa a declarar?
passenger	Não tenho nada.
official	O senhor quer abrir a mala, se faz favor?

Actividades

1 Fill in the gaps in this dialogue at the airport. (*Answers on page 130.*)

controladora	O senhor tem .... e bilhete?
passageiro	Sim, ... [here].
controladora	Quer fumador, ou .... ?
passageiro	Não fumador, por favor.
controladora	.... [will you] passar as suas
	.... [suitcases] à balança, se faz favor? [Only]
	.... tem estas?
passageiro	Só, [and] .... este saco que [I'm going]
	.... levar comigo.

controladora [OK] .... O vôo BA123 para
.... [Italy] vai ter um atraso de
.... [35 minutes]. Pode passar para a
[gate] .... número .... [fifteen].

2 Listen to the announcement of three flights in the airport and mark on the table the missing information. (*Answers on page 130.*)

	flight no.	destination	delay?	how long?	gate no.
1.					
2.					
3.					

3 You are going to be the check-in attendant, dealing with a passenger. Let the prompts below guide you. (*Answers on the recording and on page 130.*)

   1. Do you have passport and ticket, sir?
   2. Do you want smoking or non-smoking?
   3. Do you want to pass your suitcase on to the scales?
   4. Do you only have this one?
   5. Flight TAP 567 to Faro is going to have a delay of 20 minutes.
   6. You can pass to gate number 14.

Língua

Quer ('do you want', 'would you like'), is also used to mean 'would you mind ...', as you saw in the dialogue:

Quer passar a sua mala?	Would you mind passing your suitcase?
O senhor quer abrir a mala?	Would you mind opening the suitcase?

De interesse

Lisbon is a rapidly evolving city, whose international airport has recently undergone a huge overhaul and expansion to increase its capacity to deal with growing business and tourist visitors to this cosmopolitan capital.

53 Directions

Getting around the airport

Vocabulário

ao chegar	on arriving
podia ...?	could you ...?
alugar	to rent
o aluguer	the hire, rent
o carrossel	baggage reclaim
os lavabos	the toilets
uma pergunta	a question
um automóvel	a car
um carrinho	a trolley
por ali	over there
em frente	in front, opposite
em segundo lugar	secondly

Diálogo

tourist	Faz favor. Podia me dizer onde são os lavabos no aeroporto?
woman	Claro. O senhor passa por ali, em frente, vira à direita, e vai ver os lavabos mesmo em frente.
tourist	Muito obrigado. Agora, mais duas perguntas. Primeiro, preciso de alugar um automóvel e, em segundo lugar, preciso dum carrinho para trazer as malas do carrossel.
woman	Bom, há várias companhias de carros de aluguer por ali, e, depois, há carrinhos para bagagem perto da alfândega. É só virar aqui à esquerda e ao chegar a alfândega vai ver os carrinhos ao lado.
tourist	Obrigado.
woman	De nada.

Actividades

A	B
fazer	carrinho
pagar	vinho
comprar	dinheiro

1 Fill in the spaces in these sentences with a verb from Box A, or an item from Box B. Each sentence practises the verb **precisar** (to need), which you met in Unit 11. You will find one set of possible answers on page 130.

   1. Preciso de .... um jornal.
   2. Tu precisas de .... para beber.
   3. O João precisa dum ....
   4. Nós precisamos .... a conta.
   5. Os senhores precisam .... as compras.
   6. Eles precisam de ....

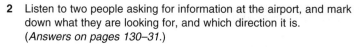

Cross reference with units:
5
17
29
45

2 Listen to two people asking for information at the airport, and mark down what they are looking for, and which direction it is. (*Answers on pages 130–31.*)

	looking for what?	where is it?
1.		
2.		

3 Imagine you are the information clerk at the airport. Two people will ask you for help. Use the prompts below to guide you through the dialogue. (*Answers on the recording and on page 131.*)

1. Of course. You pass down there, straight ahead, turn left, and you will see the car hire, right in front.
2. Of course. You just turn right here and, when you arrive at customs, you will see the toilets on the left.
3. Don't mention it.

Língua

Ao chegar means 'on arriving' 'on arrival' 'when you arrive'. This is quite a common structure in Portuguese, and is easy to form: **ao + verb in the infinitive:**

ao pagar a conta …	on paying the bill …
ao sair da casa …	on leaving the house …
ao visitar o museu …	on visiting the museum …

Podia (or **poderia**), meaning 'could you', like **queria** and **gostava**, which you met in Unit 32, is an example of a conditional in Portuguese, in English we use 'could' and 'would', especially in polite requests, as in the dialogue.
In the example **podia me dizer** … the **me** is another pronoun, this time being the object of the verb. Object pronouns can either be 'direct', answering the question 'What?', or 'indirect', answering the question 'To whom?'. In our example **me** is indirect – 'Can you tell (it) **to me**'.

	I	*you* (fam.)	*he/she/it/you*	*we*	*they/you* (pl.)
direct	**me**	**te**	**o/a**	**nos**	**os/as**
indirect	**me**	**te**	**lhe**	**nos**	**lhes**

De interesse

All major towns have at least two or three main car-hire firms operating in them. If you intend to drive in Portugal, make sure you have a licence, insurance and permission to drive the vehicle, if it is not actually yours. Otherwise spot-traffic checks can be an ordeal.

Town amenities

Buying bus tickets at the kiosk

Vocabulário

o metro	the underground
os funiculares	the funiculars
o elevador	the lift
o motorista	the driver
os eléctricos	the trams
um módulo	a type of ticket (see **De Interesse**)
a avenida	the avenue
a forma	the form, type
(o) transporte	transport
paga	you pay
ao entrar	when you enter/get on
vale	is worth
vale a pena	it's worth it
poupa	you save

Diálogo

tourist	Bom dia, senhor. Queria saber quanto custa um bilhete de autocarro até à Avenida do Brasil.
attendant	Bom, se não tem módulos, paga ao motorista ao entrar, e a viagem custa cento e cinquenta escudos.
tourist	Que são módulos?
attendant	Pode-se comprar aqui, cada módulo vale duas viagens aqui no centro, e custa cento e dez escudos. Assim a senhora poupa dinheiro.
tourist	E pode-se usar no metro também?
attendant	No metro não, mas pode-se usar nos funiculares, nos eléctricos e no Elevador de Santa Justa na Baixa.
tourist	Que boa ideia! Já que vou estar aqui algumas semanas, vale a pena.

Actividades

1   Jane has a book of **módulos** to use on transport. Write out in full in Portuguese how much she would spend if she made the following journeys in the centre, remembering that each módulo costs 110 escudos, and each can be used for two journeys. (*Answers on page 131.*)

   1. two journeys ....

   2. five journeys ....

   3. one stop only ....

   4. seven journeys ....

   5. three journeys ....

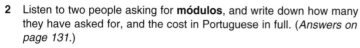

Cross reference with units:

2 Listen to two people asking for **módulos**, and write down how many they have asked for, and the cost in Portuguese in full. (*Answers on page 131.*)

	how many módulos	total cost
1.		
2.		

3 Now take part in a dialogue at a ticket kiosk. (*Answers on the recording and on page 131.*)

1. Good morning. How much is a bus ticket to the Baixa?
2. How much does a módulo cost?
3. Can one use them on the trams?
4. In that case, I would like six, please.

Língua

Pode-se is an impersonal way of saying 'you can'. You take the third (he/she) part of the verb and add **se**. It actually means 'one can', 'people can', 'it is possible' and if you have studied French, it is equivalent to the **on** form. It is used when the information given is relevant to everyone in general and not just the person addressed. Other examples you may come across include:

Precisa-se dum médico.	A doctor is needed.
Fala-se inglês.	English (is) spoken.

De interesse

Buying **módulos** is an excellent way of saving money if you intend being in a Portuguese town for any length of time.
The **Elevador de Santa Justa** is a marvellous lift designed by Eiffel. It takes people up from the lower part of Lisbon, known as the **Baixa**, to the upper part, **Bairro Alto**.

The town centre

Buying groceries

Vocabulário

provar	to try
diga lá	come on then, say then
que é isto?	what is this?
chega!	enough!
assim dá	that'll do
(o) açúcar	sugar
(a) manteiga	butter
(a) farinha	flour
(o) presunto	smoked ham
(o) queijo fresco	cottage cheese
(o) chouriço	spicy sausage
um pacote	a packet
uma caixinha	a small box/tub
um garrafão	a demijohn
meia dúzia	half a dozen
sem sal	without salt

Diálogo

Sra Brown	Boa tarde, senhor Pereira. Preciso dumas coisas.
Sr Pereira	Então, diga lá. O que quer?
Sra Brown	Quero meio quilo de açúcar, um pacote de manteiga sem sal, e um quilo de farinha.
Sr Pereira	Vai fazer um bolo?
Sra Brown	Vou, sim. O meu neto faz anos no domingo.
Sr Pereira	Precisa de mais alguma coisa?
Sra Brown	Sim. Também quero cinco fatias de presunto, uma caixinha de queijo fresco e, o que é isto aqui?
Sr Pereira	É chouriço novo da serra.
Sra Brown	Então vou levar um pouco para provar. Trezentos gramas, se faz favor. Chega! Assim dá.
Sr Pereira	Que mais?
Sra Brown	Meia dúzia de ovos e um garrafão de água.
Sr Pereira	Mais?
Sra Brown	É tudo. Obrigada.

Actividades

1   Fill in the gaps with words from the boxes. (*Answers on page 131.*)

Quero meio .... de farinha, uma dúzia de..............., um .... de água, manteiga sem .... e um .... de .... fresco.

garrafão	queijo	sal	quilo	pouco	ovos

2 Here is Ana's **lista de compras** (shopping list). As she goes through her list on the recording, tick off everything she asks for. You will find one item is overlooked. Which one? (*Answers on page 131.*)

a dozen eggs
half kilo butter
two tubs of cottage cheese
demi-john of water
three slices of smoked ham
200 g spicy sausage
kilo of flour
packet of sugar

3 Now take part in a dialogue at the grocer's, following the prompts on the recording to guide you. (*Answers on the recording and on page 131.*)

   1. Good morning, Mr Silva. I need some things.
   2. I want a kilo of flour and 300g of spicy sausage.
   3. Yes, I also want half a kilo of sugar.
   4. A dozen eggs and a packet of butter.
   5. That's all. Thanks.

Língua

It is quite acceptable, with people who are not complete strangers, to use **quero** (I want) instead of **queria** (I would like). It is not considered impolite.

De interesse

Chouriço is a very popular, spicy, continental-style sausage, found in various Portuguese meals, including the delicious shredded kale soup – **caldo verde**.

Personal choices

Favourite modes of transport

Vocabulário

de avião	by plane
de táxi	by taxi
de moto	by motorbike
... demais	too ...
fico enjoado	I get sick
dá-me	gives me
apanho	I catch
(ir) ao estrangeiro	(to go) abroad
como vais para ...?	how do you get to ...?
tenho medo	I'm afraid
rápido	fast
confortável	comfortable
eficiente	efficient
lento	slow
saudável	healthy
barato	cheap
a hora de ponta	rush hour

Diálogo

Pedro Ana, gostas de viajar de avião?

Ana Adoro. É muito rápido, confortável e eficiente. Quando vou ao estrangeiro sempre vou de avião.

Pedro Não preferes ir de barco?

Ana Não. Acho o barco demasiado lento, e sempre fico enjoada. Acho um pouco caro também.

Pedro Também não gosto tanto de barcos. Como vais para o trabalho? Vais de carro?

Ana Às vezes. Mas a hora de ponta dá-me dor de cabeça, então às vezes apanho o autocarro, ou vou a pé.

Pedro Ir a pé é muito saudável e barato, mas lento demais para mim. Quando tenho pressa vou de táxi. Aos fins de semana gosto de passear de moto.

Ana As motos vão muito rápido para mim. Tenho medo de viajar assim. Prefiro andar a cavalo.

Actividades

1 Match up the pictures both to the labels and to one of the words in the boxes, which best describes each mode of transport. (*Answers on page 131.*)

1. 2. 3. 4. 5.

a) de barco **b)** de carro **c)** de táxi **d)** de moto **e)** de avião

rápido	barato	caro	lento	eficiente	confortável

2 Listen to two people say what their favourite and least favourite means of transport is, and why, and fill in the table below. (*Answers on page 131.*)

	favourite	reason	least favourite	reason
1.				
2.				

3 Now take part in a discussion on the tape about transport. (*Answers on the recording and on page 131.*)

  1. I love it. It's comfortable and cheap.
  2. No, I think the plane is too expensive for me.
  3. Sometimes I go by bus, or sometimes on foot.
  4. I don't like travelling by motorbike – it's too fast for me.

Língua

Modes of transport are conveyed by **de + transport**, except for **a pé** and **a cavalo**.
Demasiado and **demais** both mean 'too'. **Demasiado** is placed before the adjective, and **demais** after:

> **Esta blusa é demasiado cara.**
> **Esta blusa é cara demais.**   This blouse is too expensive.

Often people just use the word **muito** (very):

> **Esta blusa é muito cara para mim**. This blouse is very/too expensive for me.

De interesse

Travelling around in Portugal is becoming easier, as new highway infrastructures now link the major cities on main routes, and comfortable express trains have been introduced between Oporto, Lisbon and the Algarve.

Holidays

Talking about a cultural holiday

Vocabulário

voltou	you've returned
acabo de voltar	I've just returned
havia/houve	there was/there were
achei	I found, thought
tantas coisas	so many things
realmente	really
cultural	cultural
culturais	cultural (pl.)
interessante	interesting
antigo	old
magnífico	magnificent
uma exposição	an exhibition
o século	the century
(a) arte	art
um panorama	a panoramic view
(as) casas de fado	fado houses
a catedral	the cathedral
as catedrais	the cathedrals
o jardim botânico	the botanical garden

Diálogo

Júlia	Olá, João. Então, já voltou das férias?
João	Sim, acabo de voltar. Foi uma semana óptima.
Júlia	O que fez?
João	Fui a Lisboa e passei a semana a fazer coisas culturais.
Júlia	Foi ao Museu Gulbenkian?
João	Fui, sim. Havia uma exposição de pinturas do século dezoito, que achei muito interessante. Também visitei o Museu de Arte Antiga.
Júlia	Foi ao Castelo de São Jorge?
João	Só passei uma hora lá – não houve tempo para fazer tudo. Gostei muito do castelo – havia um panorama magnífico da cidade.
Júlia	Lisboa é uma cidade realmente bonita.
João	Há tantas coisas para fazer – as Casas de Fado, as catedrais e palácios, o Jardim Botânico, o teatro. Na verdade, precisa-se dum mês para ver tudo.

Actividades

1 Fill in the spaces with the correct past form of the verbs in brackets. You may need to revise Unit 45. (*Answers on page 131.*)

   1. Eu (ir) .... ao castelo.
   2. O José (passar) .... uma semana em Lisboa.
   3. Eles (visitar) .... o museu.
   4. Tu (gostar) .... do Jardim Botânico?
   5. A senhora (ver) .... uma exposição.

2 Listen to three people talking about the places they have visited, when, and how much time they spent there. Make a note on the table below. (*Answers on page 131.*)

	where?	when?	how long?
1.			
2.			
3.			

3 Take part in a dialogue about some cultural activities you have participated in. (*Answers on the recording and on page 131.*)

1. I went to London and spent the week doing cultural things.
2. Yes, I did. There was an exhibition of paintings from the 16th century.
3. I only spent two hours there. There wasn't time to do everything.
4. Yes, there are so many things to do.

Língua

Havia/houve means 'there was' and 'there were', and are the equivalents of **há** in the past. **Houve** is often used in time expressions, and **havia** in giving descriptions. The dialogue contains more examples of words ending in **-l**, which form their plural in **-is**: **cultural/culturais**; **catedral/catedrais**. Both nouns and adjectives work in this way. Try to learn these as you go along, and be aware that irregularities also occur.

When talking about centuries, ordinal numbers are used up to ten (**século**: **primeiro, segundo, terceiro, quarto, quinto, sexto, sétimo, oitavo, nono, décimo**) and cardinal numbers thereafter (**século: onze, treze,** etc).

De interesse

The **Casas de Fado** are where you will hear typical Portuguese fado music. They are mostly found in Lisbon, Oporto and Coimbra, and are often restaurants. When the singer, flanked by her (or his) two guitarists, is ready to sing, the lights will be dimmed, and it is etiquette to listen in silence. If the singer is particularly good, on the penultimate line of the song, which rises to a crescendo, it is practice to shout out '**Ó, fadista**', in recognition of their skill.

 **The weather**

Talking about yesterday's weather

Vocabulário

esteve	it was
não pude	I couldn't, I was not able
chovia/estava a chover	it was raining
nevar	to snow
baixou	went down
gelar	to freeze
espalhava-se	was spreading/scattering
eu tive	I had
(as) trovoadas	thunder
(os) relâmpagos	lightning
(a) tempestade	storm
(uma) geada	(a) frost
o lixo	the rubbish
feio	bad/ugly
horrível	awful
tanto ... que	so much ... that
quem me dera	if only I could ...

 ## Diálogo

Miguel Que dia feio esteve ontem! Não pude sair.

Lumen Eu sei. Foi horrível. De manhã chovia e depois começou a nevar também.

Miguel Depois do almoço havia muito vento e o lixo espalhava-se todo pela rua.

Lumen O tempo começou a ficar muito mau – com trovoadas e relâmpagos. Eu tive muito medo.

Miguel Era uma verdadeira tempestade. À noite a temperatura baixou, e começou a gelar. Creio que hoje vamos ter geada.

Lumen Quem me dera viver num país quente!

Actividades

1 Match the pictures to the captions. (*Answers on page 131.*)

a)   b)   c)   d)   e)

1. geada **2.** relâmpagos **3.** chovia **4.** trovoadas **5.** neve

2 You will hear two people saying what kind of weather there was on certain days. Fill in the table with the relevant information. (*Answers on page 131.*)

	day	weather
1.		
2.		

3 Take part in a dialogue about yesterday's weather. (*Answers on the recording and on page 131.*)

1. I know. I couldn't get out. It was very windy.
2. I think we'll have frost today.
3. If only I could live in a tropical country!

Língua

Often when talking about past weather, we look at what was happening throughout certain periods of time, and in Portuguese we use a past tense of the verb, known as the 'imperfect' which is different to the one you have already been introduced to.

imperfect	*continuous meaning*
Havia vento, neve.	There was wind, snow
Chovia/estava a chover.	It was raining.

Compare these examples with the past tense you have already learned:

Ontem choveu.	Yesterday it rained.
Esteve muito frio.	It was very cold.

This tense describes a 'fixed', single action, and not a continuous one as in the **imperfect**.

De interesse

In the winter, the region of **Serra da Estrela** in Portugal, situated in the middle of the country and towards the Spanish border, is covered in snow, and has its own winter ski resort.

59 III health

Dealing with an accident

Vocabulário

(os) serviços de emergência	Emergency services
um acidente	an accident
uma ambulância	an ambulance
os bombeiros	the fire service
(o) ponto de referência	reference point
(as) ligaduras	bandages
(os) pensos	plasters
houve	there has been
precisamos	we need
chocaram	bumped (into each other)
ajudar	to help
venha depressa	hurry up!
exactamente	exactly
feridas	injured

Diálogo

woman	Serviços de emergência. Diga o que quer.
man	Houve um acidente. Precisamos duma ambulância.
woman	Onde aconteceu o acidente?
man	Estamos na esquina da Rua Camões com a Rua da Sé.
woman	E qual é o problema exactamente?
man	Dois carros chocaram um com o outro. Há três pessoas feridas. Temos um médico aqui a ajudar com ligaduras e pensos, mas isto é uma emergência.
woman	Precisam dos bombeiros também?
man	Não sei, provavelmente.
woman	Qual é o seu nome, por favor?
man	Chamo-me Roberto dos Santos. Trabalho perto daqui na farmácia.
woman	E qual é o ponto de referência mais próximo?
man	É o Banco Sol na Rua Camões. Estamos bem perto. Venha depressa, por favor.

Actividades

1 Read the dialogue again, and say whether these statements are **verdadeiro** or **falso**. (*Answers on page 131.*)

	V	F
1. Precisa-se duma ambulância.	☐	☐
2. O acidente aconteceu na Rua do Sol.	☐	☐
3. Três carros chocaram-se.	☐	☐
4. Há pessoas feridas.	☐	☐
5. O Sr dos Santos trabalha no banco.	☐	☐

2 Listen to someone giving details of an accident and fill in the table below. (*Answers on page 131.*)

where is accident?	how many injured?	name of caller	point of reference

3 Now imagine you have to contact the emergency services about an accident. Follow the prompts below. (*Answers on the recording and on page 131.*)

1. There's been an accident. We need an ambulance.
2. On the corner of Sé Street and Brazil Street. There are five people injured.
3. (Give your own name.)
4. The Mendes Chemist. Hurry up, please!

Língua

The word **problema**, although ending in **-a**, is actually masculine. There are a number of words which do not conform to the normal rules of gender, such as **o chá** (the tea); **o telegrama** (the telegram), **o cinema** (the cinema). Keep an eye out for them as you go along in your learning.

Venha depressa! (hurry up!) is an example of a polite command as you learned in **Unit 29**. Other irregular commands you may come across include:

fazer	to do/make	faça!	do/make!
ver	to see	veja!	see!
pôr	to put	ponha!	put!

You have also seen: **traga** (bring), **dê** (give) and **venha** (come).

Houve is the past tense of the verb **haver** used for definite, single actions, meaning 'there was'/'there has been'. You also know **há**, 'there is'/'there are', and **havia**, 'there was/were' (Continuous past).

De interesse

The emergency phone number in Portugal is 112, and it is a free number. Talking on the phone in any other language is always difficult, so explain you are foreign, and ask the operator to speak slowly. Try to give as much information about the accident as possible, including the nearest reference points.

Time

Departure and arrival times

Vocabulário

não tenho certeza	I'm not certain/sure
atrasado	late/delayed
à espera de	waiting for
a sala de espera	the waiting room
o check-in	the check-in
a visita	the visit
partiremos	we shall depart
partirá	it will depart
chegaremos	we shall arrive
chegarão	you will arrive
espero que tenha gostado	I hope you (have) enjoyed
aceita?	will you accept?
aceito	I accept
voltarei	I shall return
com muito gosto	with much pleasure
boa viagem!	bon voyage!
até à próxima	see you next time
obrigada por tudo	thanks for everything
um dia destes	one of these days

Diálogo

António	Então, Anne, a que horas vai partir?
Anne	Não tenho a certeza, António. Creio que está atrasado. Espere aqui um momento, vou perguntar.

Anne	Por favor, estou à espera do vôo BA 335 para a Inglaterra. Sabe a que horas partiremos?
attendant	Este vôo partirá às vinte e quinze. Houve um atraso de quarenta minutos por causa do vento.
Anne	E a que horas chegaremos lá?
attendant	Provavelmente chegarão às vinte e duas e trinta. Já fez o check-in?
Anne	Já.
attendant	Então, pode passar para a sala de espera.

António	Espero que a Anne tenha gostado da visita a Portugal. Aceita uma pequena lembrança do nosso país?
Anne	Aceito, sim, com muito gosto … Ah! um galo de Barcelos – o símbolo de Portugal. Muito obrigada. Gostei imenso de cá estar.
António	Boa viagem, e até à próxima!
Anne	Adeus, e obrigada por tudo. Voltarei um dia destes …

Actividades

1 Fill in the gaps in these sentences. (*Answers on page 131.*)

1
.... partirá às .... (10.15)

2
.... chegará às .... (21.20)

3
.... chegará às .... (03.40)

4
.... partirá às .... (08.13)

5
.... partirá às .... (17.50)

2 Listen to two people asking about departure/arrival times when travelling. Note down any delay and the reasons for it. (*Answers on page 131.*)

	transport	departure	delay?	how long?	why?	arrival
1.						
2.						

3 You are now going to be a ticket clerk at a port. Follow the prompts below. (*Answers on the recording and on page 131.*)

1. The next boat to Brazil will leave at 10.20. **2.** There has been a delay of two hours because of the bad weather. **3.** The boat will probably arrive at 8.30 am on Thursday. **4.** Have you checked in yet? **5.** Well then, you can pass to the waiting room.

Língua

The future tense, although often replaced by the more colloquial use of the verb **ir** 'to go' (I'm going to …) is, nevertheless, handy to know. The formation is the same for all verbs. The following endings are simply added to the verb infinitive:

eu	tu	ele/ela/você/o sr	nós	eles/elas/vocês/os srs
+ei	+ás	+á	+emos	+ão
chegarei	chegarás	chegará	chegaremos	chegarão
entrarei	entrarás	entrará	entraremos	entrarão
partirei	partirás	partirá	partiremos	partirão

There are three exceptions – **fazer** (to do), **trazer** (to bring), **dizer** (to say) – and their forms are:

farei	farás	fará	faremos	farão
trarei	trarás	trará	traremos	trarão
direi	dirás	dirá	diremos	dirão

De interesse

The Barcelos cockerel is a symbol of peace and harmony. Legend has it that an innocent man was condemned to die, until a roasted cockerel stood up and crowed to prove his innocence. From that day forwards, the cockerel has been used to symbolise the spirit of these very generous people.

Portugal, Madeira, and the Azores are great destinations for short, or long-term visits. The people will extend a warm welcome to visitors, both old and young alike, and now that you can speak some Portuguese, you will find a whole new world awaiting you on arrival.

Answers to exercises

1 1 **2.** Chamo-me Françoise. Sou de Paris. **3.** Chamo-me Mark. Sou de Londres. **4.** Chamo-me Helga. Sou de Berlim. **2** 1. Maria/Faro; **2.** Miguel/Lisboa; **3.** Eduarda/Lagos **3** 1. Bom dia. Chamo-me Frank. **2.** Sou inglês. Sou de Lancaster. **3.** Igualmente.

2 1 **1.** uma água mineral; **2.** um pastel de nata; **3.** um café e uma empada de galinha **2** 1. empada/café; **2.** água mineral/pastel de nata **3** 1. Queria uma empada de galinha. **2.** Sim, queria uma água mineral, se faz favor. **3.** Fresca. **4.** Com gás.

3 1 **1.** b); **2.** c); **3.** a) **2** 1. 2 people/4 nights/1 double; **2.** 5 people/8 nights/2 doubles and 1 single **3** 1. Bom dia. Tem quartos vagos? **2.** Para uma. **3.** Para cinco.

4 1 **2.** Não, não é. **3.** É sim. **4.** Não, não é. **2** 1. V; **2.** F; **3.** F **3** 1. Leva dezassete minutos. **2.** Leva treze minutos. **3.** Leva dezanove minutos.

5 1 **1.** sim; **2.** não **2** Turn left, then straight ahead, next turn right and carry on, then turn right and the tourist office is on the left of the Square. **3** 1. Desculpe, há um posto de Turismo aqui? **2.** Fica muito longe? **3.** Pode repetir mais devagar, se faz favor? **4.** Obrigado/a.

6 1 **1.** c); **2.** b); **3.** a) **2** 1. Braga/Monday **2.** Oporto/Sunday **3** 1. Bom dia. **2.** Têm informações sobre o Porto? **3.** Posso fazer reservas para excursões aqui? **4.** Para Fátima. **5.** Queria dois bilhetes para a quarta-feira.

7 1 **1.** b); **2.** d); **3.** e); **4.** a); **5.** c) **2** 1. bookshop in the Square; **2.** butcher's on the corner, next to grocer's. **3** 1. Desculpe, onde é que posso comprar um livro? **2.** Obrigada. Ah, outra coisa – onde é que posso comprar carne? **3.** Obrigadinha.

8 1 **1.** d); **2.** a); **3.** e); **4.** b); **5.** c) **2** José likes Braga, Lisboa, Albufeira; Ana likes Lisboa and Porto, but not Albufeira. **3** 1. Gosto muito – há muito para ver. **2.** Não, não gosto muito de Paris. **3.** Sim, prefiro Madrid porque há muito para fazer.

9 1 **2.** O hotel é pequeno. **3.** Os sapatos são bonitos. **4.** As laranjas são baratas. **5.** A camisa é cara. **2** Bom dia; cá; negócios; férias; férias; férias; é, não; caro; são; bonitas; visitar; ver; então **3** 1. Sim, estou, Gosto muito de Portugal. **2.** Estou de férias, porque não faz tanto calor e é muito bonito. **3.** Pretendo visitar Évora.

10 1 **1.** a); **2.** e); **3.** d); **4.** c); **5.** b) **2** Guarda: very hot, no wind, cloudy; Lisboa: good weather, blue sky, windy; Setúbal: not very hot; windy, cloudy, no blue sky. **3** 1. Ainda bem! Queria cinco gelados, se faz favor. **2.** Três sorvetes de morango e dois gelados. **3.** Sim, o céu está azul e não há vento.

11 1 **2.** Este/ This sky is blue. **3.** Estes/ These shoes are pretty. **4.** Este/ This man is good-looking. **5.** Esta/ This lady is fair. **6.** Estes/ These shoes are not expensive. **2** 1. factor 10/ twice a day; **2.** factor 16/ once a day. **3** 1. Temos sim. Recomendo o factor número quinze. Precisa de usar três vezes por dia. **2.** Temos sim. Recomendo o factor número doze. Precisa de usar uma vez por dia.

12 1 **1.** c); **2.** a); **3.** d); **4.** b) **2** 31; 62; 57; 92; 38; 49; 66; 55 **3** 1. Trinta e quatro minutos. **2.** Sessenta e um minutos. **3.** Noventa e sete minutos.

13 **1** 1. English, German, French;
2. not French, Portuguese; 3. German
2 1. German **, Portuguese *;
2. French -, English -, German X;
3. French *, German *, Portuguese **;
4. French **, English *, German X.
3 1. Bom dia. Estou bem, obrigado/a.
2. E como está o senhor?
3. Obrigado/a. O senhor fala inglês?
4. Falo um pouco de alemão e também
um pouco de francês.

14 **1** 1. é, fatia, bolo; 2. a, com,
sandes; 3. pode, uma **2** 1. V; 2. F;
3. F **3** 1. Para mim, uma bica e uma
fatia de bolo de chocolate. 2. O que tem
de sanduiches? 3. Bom, para mim pode
ser uma de ovo, se faz favor.

15 **1** 1. c); 2. b); 3. d); 4. a)
2 1. double room, with bath, with
breakfast 2. single, with bath, no
breakfast **3** 1. Boa tarde, queria
reservar um quarto de casal. 2. Para o
dia vinte e sete de Janeiro. 3. Duas.
4. Com, se faz favor.

16 **1** 1. b); 2. d); 3. a); 4. e); 5. c)
2 1. 1st class 2. platform 8 3. 2,185
escudos 4. 12 mins **3** 1. Queria um
bilhete de ida e volta para Braga, se faz
favor. 2. Primeira. Quanto custa?
3. Qual é a linha?

17 **1** a) em frente do b) na praça
c) detrás do d) ao lado do **2** speaker 2
3 1. Onde fica o banco? 2. Desculpe,
pode repetir mais devagar, se faz favor?
3. Fica longe? 4. Muito obrigada/o.

18 **1** 1. f); 2. d); 3. a); 4. b); 5. c);
6. e) **2** 6 cheques, £120, Sheraton,
Rua Boavista 62, Lisboa **3** 1. Queria
trocar estes travellers cheques.
2. Cinco, de vinte libras cada. 3. Aqui
está. 4. Hotel Palácio, Rua Principal,
número trinta e seis, Nazaré.

19 **1** 1. c); 2. a); 3. e); 4. b); 5. d)
2 Size 44; colours shown: blue, yellow;
prices: blue – 2,850 and yellow – 2,700;

colour chosen: blue. **3** 1. Bom dia, queria
comprar uma blusa. 2. É trinta e oito.
Tem alguma coisa em verde? 3. Posso
experimentar aquela? 4. Quanto custa?

20 **1** 1. b); 2. d); 3. a); 4. c); 5. e)
2 José: sometimes, often, sometimes.
Paula: never, often, always **3** 1. Nem
sempre, às vezes faço as compras no
supermercado. 2. Quase nunca vou à
feira. 3. Em geral, faço as compras lá
nas quintas, mas esta semana ando
muito ocupado.

21 **1** 2. summer/Japan 3. spring/
Germany 4. winter/Portugal 5. autumn/
Switzerland **2** Greece, nowhere,
England, Switzerland **3** 1. Passo as
férias de primavera na França porque a
paisagem é muito linda. 2. Nunca tiro
férias no verão. 3. No outono gosto de
visitar Portugal quando a costa está
mais calma.

22 **1** 1. b); 2. d); 3. a); 4. c); 5. e)
2 1. Cascais 2. Sagres **3** 1. Que
bom. Dois pacotes, se faz favor. 2. Tem
razão, faz frio e o céu está nublado.
3. Às vezes, mas este ano há mais
vento. 4. Hoje está um dia péssimo para
a praia.

23 **1** 1. cabeça, c); 2. garganta,
a); 3. constipada, b). **2** male
3 1. Obrigado/a, estou constipado/a.
2. Estou a tomar aspirina porque tenho
uma dor de cabeça. 3. Boa ideia.
Também tenho uma dor de garganta e
estou muito cansado/a.

24 **1** 1. d); 2. a); 3. c); 4. b); 5. e)
2 1. museum, 9.30am, 6.40pm,
12–2.15; 2. bakers, 7am, 1.45pm, not
mentioned. **3** 1. Abre às oito e vinte
da manhã. 2. Fecha ao meio dia e meia
para o almoço. 3. Depois, reabre à uma
e um quarto.

25 **1** 1. a mulher 2. casados
3. o marido 4. a mãe 5. o pai 6. o filho
7. a filha 8. filhos 9. a irmã 10. o irmão

2 1. married, 2 children, no brothers; 2 sisters **2.** not married, no children, 3 brothers; 1 sister **3 1.** Ele fala inglês. **2.** O senhor vive na Suécia? **3.** Elas chamam-se Mary e Jean. **4.** O irmão dele vive na França. **5.** O marido dela chama-se José.

26

1 1. c); **2.** d); **3.** b); **4.** e); **5.** a) **2** sopa de legumes, caldo verde, frango piri-piri, leitão, mousse de chocolate, gelado de baunilha, vinho branco **3 1.** A lista, se faz favor. **2.** Para começar, um caldo verde e uma sopa de legumes. **3.** Para mim, as sardinhas assadas e, para o meu irmão, o bacalhau. **4.** O que tem? **5.** Duas saladas de fruta. **6.** Uma garrafa do vinho da casa. **7.** Tinto, obrigado/a.

27

1 José, dos Santos Pereira; 25 de Março de 1963; Castelo Branco, Rua S. Pedro, 10. 3°esq. Braga, BI372201568BJL; Português, terça-feira, 10 de Junho de 1998. **2** 48 (T) **3** (your name), (your surname), (your date of birth), (your place of birth), (your address), (your passport number), (your nationality).

28

1 b) quinze c) Lisboa d) Braga **2** Albufeira, every 20 min; 10.35, direct, 12.40. **3 1.** A que horas há uma camioneta para Viana? **2.** E a que horas parte a próxima? **3.** É directa? **4.** Quanto custa um bilhete?

29

1 1. b); **2.** d); **3.** a); **4.** c); **5.** e) **2** Directions: turn right, pass in front of ticket office, go up to steps. Go up and over footbridge. Descend and turn right. Platform for France is the second one along. Platform number 8. **3 1.** O comboio para Braga sai de que linha? **2.** E para chegar lá? **3.** Espere um momento, já estou perdido/a! **4.** O senhor é muito gentil, obrigado/a.

30

1 1. b) cento e cinquenta; **2.** d) duzentos e trinta; **3.** a) quinhentos;

4. c) quinhentos e vinte e cinco; **5.** e) quinhentos e cinquenta e cinco **2** Spain, 2205, 75288, sr González **3** Queria fazer uma chamada a cobrar no destino. (country) (town code) (phone number) (name of person you want to talk to) (your name).

31

1 1. c); **2.** a); **3.** d); **4.** b); **5.** e) **2** They buy: 2kg pears, 2 cauliflowers, 250g mushrooms, 3kg potatoes, 1kg oranges, $\frac{1}{2}$ kg tomatoes. Not available today: lettuce. **3 1.** Bom dia. Tem cogumelos hoje? **2.** Dê-me/queria duzentos e cinquenta gramas. **3.** Também queria meio quilo de peras, três alfaces, e seis quilos de batatas. **4.** Tem melão? **5.** Então dê-me um quilo de maçãs. **6.** A como é a laranja hoje? **7.** Dê-me dois quilos, obrigado/a.

32

1 1. cinema/ver **2.** bar/tomamos **3.** jantar **4.** ir/museu **5.** passar/boate **2** Eduardo prefers on Sat: relax in bar, eat in, go dancing; on Sun: see film. Paula prefers on Sat: see film, stroll in centre; on Sun: eat out, relax in bar. **3 1.** Gostaria de tomar uma bebida num bar. **2.** Preferia jantar fora. **3.** Não, preferia ir ver um filme.

33

1 1. vamos/ visitar/ no ano que vem **2.** (ela) vai/ ficar/ na semana que vem **3.** no mês que vem/ vais/ ver **4.** vou/ viajar/ no ano que vem **5.** na semana que vem/ (eles) vão/ passear **2 1.** next week/ see a friend/ Holland **2.** next month/ pottery course/ library **3 1.** No ano que vem eu e a minha família vamos visitar a Dinamarca no inverno. **2.** Onde vai passar as férias no mês que vem? **3.** No mês que vem vou ficar em casa e fazer um curso de português.

34

1 1. F; **2.** V; **3.** F; **4.** F; **5.** V **2** Madrid 12°; London 3°; Paris 8°; Amsterdam 0°; Rome 14° **3 1.** Boa noite, aqui temos a previsão do tempo para hoje para Inglaterra. **2.** Na região do norte, o céu vai estar nublado com vento moderado. **3.** As temperaturas vão chegar a dezoito graus no sul. **4.** A qualidade do ar observada em Londres é razoável.

35 **1** 1. arm 2. foot 3. eyes 4. stomach 5. teeth. **2** has pain in legs and head, has hurt back.
3 1. Bom dia. Não me sinto muito bem. 2. Tenho uma dor de cabeça e doem-me os dentes. 3. Ontem magoei a cabeça e cortei o dedo. 4. Nos olhos, não, mas dói-me o estômago.

36 **1** 1. d); 2. c); 3. a); 4. e); 5. b)
2 1. 8.15 2. 12.00 3. 7.00 4. 11.10
3 1. Ontem de manhã fui para o trabalho cedo e voltei a casa para almoçar à uma e meia. 2. Depois, saí para ir à biblioteca. 3. Fui a um restaurante com um amigo. 4. Comi frango, bolo de amêndoa, e bebi meia garrafa de vinho branco. 5. Eram onze e um quarto quando cheguei em casa.

37 **1** 1. c); 2. a); 3. d); 4. e)
2 1. José; designer; doesn't mention 2. Ana Maria; doesn't mention, school 3. Paulo; civil servant; Lisbon **3** 1. Boa tarde, Teresa. 2. Sou desenhador. Trabalho numa empresa internacional em Lisboa. 3. Sim, gosto muito. 4. A minha mulher trabalha numa escola. É secretária. 5. O que é que faz, Teresa?

38 **1** queríamos, salada, meia-dose, arroz, traga, sobremesa, fruta, cafés **2** Dish 1 has cod, garlic, carrots, olives, tomato, rice; 2 has pork, garlic, rice, onion, green pepper, olives Joan can eat dish no. 2. **3** 1. Sim. queríamos o bacalhau na cataplana e uma feijoada. 2. Meia dose dá para uma pessoa? 3. Então, só meia dose do bacalhau. 4. Os pratos vêm com batatas fritas ou salada? 5. Então, traga uma salada também, por favor.

39 **1** 1. e); 2. b); 3. a); 4. d); 5. f); 6. e) **2** 1. sala de estar 2. cozinha

3. jardim **4.** quarto **5.** casa de banho **6.** W.C. **3** 1. os meus quartos 2. a tua casa 3. o seu jardim 4. as suas cozinhas 5. a sala de estar dele 6. a sala de jantar dela.

40 **1** 1. e); 2. f); 3. d); 4. a); 5. c)
2 1. 4-star fill tank; 5 litres oil 2. 20 litres diesel; $\frac{1}{2}$ litre oil **3** 1. Bom dia. Enche o depósito, se faz favor. 2. Normal sem chumbo, se faz favor. 3. Tem óleo? 4. Dois litros. 5. Vendem mapas da região? 6. Está bem. Quanto é? 7. Obrigada/o. Adeus.

41 **1** 1. b); 2. d); 3. a); 4. c); 5. e)
2 Lisboa; no; left at lights; 200km
3 1. Para Viseu? Não é por aqui. 2. Tem que voltar para trás até aos semáforos, e depois virar à esquerda e tomar a estrada para Guarda. 3. Logo vai ver uma rotunda, – é só seguir o sinal que diz Viseu, e pronto, chegará. 4. Sim, é um pouco longe. Viseu fica a uns noventa e cinco quilómetros daqui.

42 **1** desportos; piscina; hípico; cavalo; campo; ténis; sócio; jogar; piquenique; parque **2** swimming; park; football; golf course; picnic areas **3** 1. Bom dia. Tem informações sobre os desportos na cidade? 2. A piscina abre todos os dias? 3. Tem que ser sócio para jogar golfe? 4. Onde fica o campo de golfe? 5. Obrigado/a.

43 **1** 1. preto 2. vermelhas 3. lindos 4. pesados 5. nacional
2 cockerel: yes, red, orange, white; tablecloths: yes; white, orange; tiles: yes; not specified; tile panels: yes; not specified shawl: no **3** 1. Bom dia. Estou à procura duma lembrança típica de Portugal para a minha filha. O que recomenda? 2. Tem xailes pretos? 3. Tem azulejos? 4. Não quero nada muito pesado. 5. Boa ideia. Também vou levar um xaile preto.

44 **1** nadar/ ler/ pintar/ andar/

ouvir música   **2** 1. likes golf, swimming, indoor activities like reading; dislikes music **2.** likes painting, sports, like golf; dislikes bike riding **3** 1. Gosto de andar de bicicleta e de nadar. **2.** A bicicleta. **3.** Às vezes gosto de ouvir música. **4.** O meu marido gosta de ler. Detesta os desportos.

45 1 1. c); **2.** f); **3.** a); **4.** d); **5.** e); **6.** b)   **2** 1. Italy; husband; liked; Rome **2.** France; didn't like; south and Paris **3.** Brazil; Pedro; liked; Rio **3** 1. O ano passado fui a Madeira com a minha família. **2.** Gostámos muito, mas a minha mulher não gostou da comida. **3.** Sim, visitámos Funchal e vimos as levadas. **4.** Sim, mas também foi um pouco cansativo.

46 1 1. V; **2.** F; **3.** F; **4.** F; **5.** V **2** Winter: N. hot; S. quite cold; E. not mentioned; W. more rain. Summer: N. tropical, hot, lots of rain; S. less hot, dry; E. humid, hot; W. very dry. **3** 1. Nem sempre Maria. O nosso clima cá e bastante variável. **2.** No inverno é frio no norte e chove muito. 3. No verão é quente no sul, e bastante quente no norte. **4.** É um pouco, mas o clima em Portugal na primavera e no verão é melhor. **5.** Não gosto dum clima demasiado quente, então o clima da Grã-Bretanha é perfeito para mim.

47 1 1. um tornozelo partido **2.** um médico **3.** gesso **4.** uma radiografia **5.** um pulso inchado **2** 1. knee; broken; yes; 7 weeks; yes; 2 months **2.** ankle; twisted; no; yes; 5 weeks   **3** 1. Preciso de ver um médico, por favor. **2.** Penso que tenho um tornozelo partido. **3.** Hoje de manhã fui atropelada por uma bicicleta. **4.** Vou ter que descansar?

48 1 1. d) **2.** b) **3.** e) **4.** a) **5.** c) **2** 1. 4:40; bookshop; – ; 5pm **2.** 12:30; baker's; – ; 2pm **3.** 7:15; butcher's; 8am; –   **3** 1. Que horas são, Sandra? **2.** Bom, ainda chegamos a tempo.

3. Às três horas. **4.** Sim, mas ainda temos que achar um lugar onde estacionar o carro. **5.** Chegámos mesmo à hora, vamos entrar.

49 1 1. c); **2.** a); **3.** d); **4.** b); **5.** e) **2** 1. Aunt; 46 **2.** Grandpa; 72 **3.** Grandson; 9   **3** 1. Paulo, venha conhecer as meus filhos. **2.** David, que é o mais velho, tem dezasseis anos e Laura, que é mais nova, tem catorze. **3.** David faz anos no dia vinte e cinco de Março e Laura fez anos a semana passada. **4.** Faço anos no dia três de Novembro.

50 1 1. b); **2.** e); **3.** a); **4.** d); **5.** g) **2** 1. spoon; missing **2.** bill; wrong **3.** glass; dirty   **3** 1. Faz favor. **2.** Faltam duas facas, e este garfo está sujo. Pode trazer outros? **3.** Outra coisa, o peru não está bom, e este copo está rachado. **4.** Acho que a conta está errada. Mandámos o peru de volta. **5.** Obrigado/a.

51 1 1. frigorífico **2.** condicionado **3.** água **4.** fecha **5.** chuveiro **6.** comida **2** 1. air conditioning; tap **2.** shower **3** 1. Não tenho nenhuma. **2.** Não tem nenhum. **3.** Não, ninguém fala. **4.** Não têm nenhuma.

52 1 passaporte; aqui; não fumador; quer; malas; só; e; vou; está bem; Itália; trinta e cinco minutos; porta; quinze   **2** 1. AF365/ Paris/ yes/ 50 mins/ 12 **2.** IB236/ Madrid/ no/ –/ 22 **3.** RG558/ Brazil/ yes/ 25 mins/ 6 **3** 1. Tem passaporte e bilhete, senhor? **2.** Quer fumador ou não fumador? **3.** Quer passar a sua mala à balança. **4.** Só tem esta? **5.** O vôo TAP567 para Faro vai ter um atraso de 20 minutos. **6.** Pode passar para a porta número catorze.

53 1 1. comprar **2.** vinho **3.** carrinho **4.** pagar **5.** fazer **6.** dinheiro **2** 1. car hire/ through here, turn right **2.** baggage reclaim/ through here,

straight ahead, near customs
3 1. Claro. A senhora passa por ali, em frente, vira à esquerda, e vai ver o aluguer de carros mesmo em frente. **2.** Claro. É só virar aqui à direita e, ao chegar à alfândega, vai ver os lavabos à esquerda. **3.** De nada.

54
1 1. cento e dez escudos **2.** duzentos e setenta e cinco **3.** cinquenta e cinco **4.** trezentos e oitenta e cinco **5.** cento e sessenta e cinco **2 1.** 5/ quinhentos e cinquenta escudos **2.** 3/ trezentos e trinta **3 1.** Bom dia. Quanto custa um bilhete de autocarro para a Baixa? **2.** Quanto custa um módulo? **3.** Pode-se usar nos eléctricos? **4.** Então, queria seis, se faz favor.

55
1 quilo; ovos; garrafão; sal; pouco; queijo **2** Ana forgets 1kg flour. **3 1.** Bom dia, Sr. Silva. Preciso dumas coisas. **2.** Quero um quilo de farinha e trezentos gramas de chouriço. **3.** Sim, também quero meio quilo de açúcar. **4.** Uma dúzia de ovos e um pacote de manteiga. **5.** É tudo, obrigada.

56
1 1. b) confortável; **2.** d) rápido; **3.** a) lento; **4.** c) caro; **5.** e) eficiente **2 1.** plane – very quick/ boat – I feel sick **2.** car – comfortable/ on foot – too slow **3 1.** Adoro. É confortável e barato. **2.** Não acho o avião demasiado caro para mim. **3.** Às vezes vou de autocarro ou, às vezes, a pé. **4.** Não gosto de viajar de moto – é rápido demais para mim.

57
1 1. fui **2.** passou **3.** visitaram

4. gostaste **5.** viu **2 1.** castle; last week; 2 hours **2.** city, art exhibition; last Sunday; 55 min **3.** botanical gardens; yesterday; $3\frac{1}{2}$ hours **3 1.** Fui a Londres e passei a semana a fazer coisas culturais. **2.** Sim, fui. Havia uma exposição de pinturas do século dezasseis. **3.** Só passei duas horas lá. Não houve tempo para fazer tudo. **4.** Sim, há tantas coisas para fazer.

58
1 1. c); **2.** a); **3.** d); **4.** b); **5.** e) **2 1.** Tuesday; very windy, rain **2.** Saturday; very bad, thunder, lightning, lot rain **3 1.** Eu sei. Não pude sair. Havia muito vento. **2.** Creio que hoje vamos ter geada. **3.** Quem me dera viver num país tropical!

59
1 1. V **2.** F **3.** F **4.** V **5.** F **2** Rua Principal; 4; Ana Mendes; Liberdade Chemist **3 1.** Houve um acidente, precisamos duma ambulância, **2.** Na esquina da Rua da Sé com a Rua do Brasil. Há cinco pessoas feridas. **3.** Chamo-me (your name). **4.** A Farmácia Mendes. Venha depressa, por favor.

60
1 1. o barco; dez e quinze **2.** o avião; vinte e uma e vinte/ nove e vinte **3.** a camioneta; três e quarenta **4.** o táxi; oito e treze **5.** a moto; dezassete e cinquenta/ cinco e cinquenta **2 1.** boat; 19:20; yes; 30 min; rain; 05:35 **2.** plane; 08:10; no;–;–; 11:35 **3 1.** O próximo barco para o Brasil partirá às dez e vinte. **2.** Houve um atraso de duas horas por causa do mau tempo. **3.** Provavelmente o barco chegará na quinta-feira às oito e trinta. **4.** Já fez o check-in? **5.** Então pode passar para a sala de espera.

Grammar Summary

Nouns

All things, objects, people are nouns; in Portuguese all nouns are either masculine or feminine.

	Masc. sing.	Fem. sing.	Masc. pl.	Fem. pl.
Regular	o barco	a casa	os livros	as mesas
Irregular	o papel	a estação	os jornais	as nuvens

Articles

These are the words for 'the' (definite article) and 'a/an', 'some' (indefinite article) that go in front of a noun, and they depend on whether the noun they go with is masculine or feminine.

	Masc. sing.	Fem. sing.	Masc. pl.	Fem. pl.
Definite	o	a	os	as
Indefinite	um	uma	uns	umas

Subject pronouns

These are the words for 'I', 'you', 'etc', who are carrying out the action of the verbs.

I	You (fam.)	He (it)	She (it)	You	We	They	You (pl.)
eu	tu	ele	ela	você/ o sr/a sra	nós	eles/ elas	vocês/ os srs/as sras

Verbs

In dictionaries, verbs are always listed in their infinitive (the 'to …' form of the verb). Portuguese infinitives fall into three groups according to their endings, eg.: **falar** (to speak), **comer** (to eat), **partir** (to leave.)

Regular verbs

		Eu	Tu	Ele/ela/você	Nós	Eles/elas/vocês
Present	**-ar**	falo	falas	fala	falamos	falam
	-er	como	comes	come	comemos	comem
	-ir	parto	partes	parte	partimos	partem
Preterite	**-ar**	falei	falaste	falou	falámos	falaram
	-er	comi	comeste	comeu	comemos	comeram
	-ir	parti	partiste	partiu	partimos	partiram
Imperfect	**-ar**	falava	falavas	falava	falávamos	falavam
	-er	comia	comias	comia	comíamos	comiam
	-ir	partia	partias	partia	partíamos	partiam
Future	**-ar**	falarei	falarás	falará	falaremos	falarão
	-er	comerei	comerás	comerá	comeremos	comerão
	-ir	partirei	partirás	partirá	partiremos	partirão

Conditional	-ar	falaria	falarias	falaria	falaríamos	falariam
	-er	comeria	comerias	comeria	comeríamos	comeriam
	-ir	partiria	partiria	partiria	partiríamos	partiriam

Progressive tense

Estar + A + Infinitive   To be doing … (at this moment)
Estou a falar.   I am speaking.

Reflexive verbs

These are joined to a reflexive pronoun ('self'), and are used either to do action to one-self, or in expressions such as '… is done'. The pronouns are:

me	**te**	**se**	**nos**	**se**
myself	*yourself*	*his/her/yourself/itself*	*ourselves*	*yourselves/themselves*

Lavo-me. I wash myself.   **Sentam-se.** They sit (themselves) down.

Ser/ Estar/ Ficar

Three ways of translating 'to be'.

SER –	**sou**	**es**	**é**	**somos**	**são**

Ser is used for: permanent situations, locations, professions, characteristics.

ESTAR –	**estou**	**estás**	**está**	**estamos**	**estão**

Estar is used for: temporary situations, locations, feelings, weather.

FICAR –	**fico**	**ficas**	**fica**	**ficamos**	**ficam**

Ficar is used for: permanent locations, changes of feelings/behaviour, to stay.

Ela é professora.	She is a teacher.
O livro está debaixo da mesa.	The chair is under the table.
As lojas ficam longe.	The shops are a long way off.

Commands
Ways of telling people to do something

	Tu	*Você (o sr/a sra)*	*Plural*
-ar verbs	fala!	fale!	falem!
-er verbs	come!	coma!	comem!
-ir verbs	parte!	parta!	partam!

Irregular verbs will have irregular command forms.

Adjectives

Adjectives describe a noun. They agree in number and gender with the noun they are describing, and are usually placed after the noun:

	Masc. sing.	Fem. sing.	Masc. pl.	Fem. pl.
Regular	amarelo	amarela	amarelos	amarelas
Irregular	bom	boa	bons	boas

a casa moderna the modern house **os livros pretos** the black books

Demonstratives

Words used for pointing at things or people (this/that/these/those):

	Masc. sing.	Fem. sing.	Masc. pl.	Fem. pl.
This/These	este	esta	estes	estas
That/Those	aquele	aquela	aqueles	aquelas

Possessives

Words which show to whom something belongs:

	Masc. sing.	Fem. sing.	Masc. pl.	Fem. pl.
my	o meu	a minha	os meus	as minhas
your (fam)	o teu	a tua	os teus	as tuas
your (polite)	o seu	a sua	os seus	as suas
our	o nosso	a nossa	os nossos	as nossas
your (pl.)	o vosso	a vossa	os vossos	as vossas
his	o.. dele	a.. dele	os...dele	as...dele
her	o...dela	a...dela	os...dela	as...dela
their	o...deles/	a...deles/	os...deles/	as...deles/
	delas	delas	delas	delas

The possessive agrees with the thing possessed, and not the possessor.

as nossas filhas our daughters **o carro dela** her car

Prepositions

These are words describing position, place, and time. Here are some of the more common ones:

em	de	por	para	em frente	atrás	debaixo
in/on	of/about	for, by	to, for	in front	behind	underneath

em cima	ao lado	ao pé	a	dentro	fora	perto
on top	next to	next to	to, at	inside	outside	near

Many of these are followed by **de** and the prepositions **de, a, em, por** combine and contract with definite and indefinite articles, thus:

	o	a	os	as	um	uma	uns	umas
a +	ao	à	aos	às				
de +	do	da	dos	das	dum	duma	duns	dumas
em +	no	na	nos	nas	num	numa	nuns	numas
por +	pelo	pela	pelos	pelas				

ao lado do banco	next to the bank
vou à igreja.	I'm going to the church.
dentro duma caixa	inside a box

por and **para**
Ways of translating 'for, to, by'

	por	para
used for:	price/sending/reason for	use/purpose/time for
also:	through/by/along	direction towards

por causa da chuva	because of the rain
para mim	for me

Negatives/Interrogatives

Some common negatives and interrogatives (question words) are:

não	**nunca**	**nada**	**ninguém**	**nenhum**	**nem**
no, not	never	nothing	no-one	nothing	not even

onde?	**quando?**	**como?**	**porquê?**	**(o) que?**	**qual?**	**quem?**
where?	when?	how?	why?	what?	which?	who?

Adverbs

These give more information about how the action of the verb is carried out:

Pode falar mais *devagar?*	Can you speak more slowly?

Suffixes

These are endings added to certain words to create specific effects. The commonest in Portuguese are:

- inho (-zinho)   Diminutive   **-ão (zão)**   Augmentative
makes a word smaller, cuter   makes a word larger, grosser

uma casinha	a little house
um garrafão	a demi-john (large bottle)

Of course, there is much more to Portuguese grammar than contained in this course. To progress, you will, at some point, need to purchase a good grammar book, so that you can learn to build up your confidence in constructing your own sentences.

Vocabulary

A **à mão**   by hand
abre   (it) opens
aberto   open
acho (que)   I think (that)
aconselhável   advisable
adeus   goodbye
adoro   I adore, love
agora   now
ainda   still, yet
ainda bem   just as well, thank
goodness
ajuda f.   help
alemão   German
alfândega f.   Customs
alguém   someone
alguma coisa   something
almoço m.   lunch
alugar   to hire
amanhã   tomorrow
amendoeiras f.   almond trees
americano   American
andar de bicicleta   to ride a bike
ano m.   year
antes de   before
antigo   old, antique
ao pé de   next to
apartamento m.   apartment, flat
aprender a   to learn to
aquela f.   that, that one
aqui   here
às vezes   sometimes
assim   and so, like this
assinar   to sign
até   until, up to, till
atraso m.   delay
atravessa   you, he, she cross(es)
atravessar   to cross
atúm m.   tuna
autocarro m.   bus
automóvel m.   car
avenida f.   avenue
azul   blue
azulejos m.   glazed tiles

B **bacalhau m.**   (salted) cod
banco m.   bank
bar m.   bar
barato   cheap
barco m.   boat

bastante   quite, enough
batatas f.   potatoes
baunilha f.   vanilla
bem   well
bem-vinda f.   welcome
biblioteca f.   library
bilhete m.   ticket
bilheteira f.   ticket office
blusa f.   blouse
boa ideia   good idea
boa noite   good evening/night
boa sorte   good luck
boa tarde   good afternoon
boas férias   have a good holiday
boate f.   nightclub
bolo m.   cake
bolsa f.   bag
bom dia   good morning
bom, boa, bons, boas   good
bombeiros m.   firemen
bonito   pretty
braço m.   arm
branco   white
breve   short, brief
bronzeador   tanning

C
cá   here
cada   each, every
café m.   cafe, coffee
calmo   peaceful
cama f.   bed
caminho m.   way, route
camioneta f.   coach
campo m.   countryside
cansado   tired
cansativo   tiring
cão m.   dog
caro   expensive
carne f.   meat
casa de banho f.   bathroom
casa f.   house
castanha f.   chestnut
castelo m.   castle
cedo   early
céu m.   sky
chá m.   tea
chamo-me   I am called
chegada f.   arrival
chega!   enough!

chuva f.   rain
chuveiro m.   shower
cidade f.   city, town
cinema m.   cinema
claro   fair-skinned
claro   of course
com certeza   certainly
com   with
comboio m.   train
começar   to begin
começou a   it began to
comércio m.   business
como está?   how are you?
como se chama?   what is your name?
comprar   to buy
confortável   comfortable
conhecer   to know (person, country)
conta f.   bill
correr   to run
costa f.   coast
cozinha f.   kitchen/cuisine
creio   I believe
creme m.   cream, lotion
crianças f.   children
cuidado   careful
cuidar de   to take care of

D daqui a …   … from here
data f.   date
dedo m.   finger
de ida   single (ticket)
de ida e volta   return (ticket)
demais   too, too much
demora f.   delay
de nada   don't mention it
dentes m.   teeth
dentro   inside
de onde é?   where are you from?
depois   after, then
depois de   after (doing)
depósito m.   petrol tank
depressa   quickly
descanso m.   rest
descongelar   to thaw
desculpe   excuse me
detesto   I hate
detrás de   behind
de urgência   emergency
devagar   slow(ly)

deveria   I, you, he, she ought to
de vez em quando   from time to time
diga   can I help? (lit. say)
(à) direita   on/ to the right
dizer   to say
dói/doem   hurts/hurt
dor f.   pain
dose f.   helping, portion

E

e   and
é   he, she, it is/ you are
elevador m.   lift
embrulhar   to wrap up
empada f.   pie, pastry
empresa f.   company
em total   in all
encontrar   to find
então   well then
entrada f.   entrance/hall
entre   between
errado   wrong
escadas f.   stairs, steps
escola f.   school
(à) esquerda   on, to the left
esquina f.   corner
essa f.   that, that one
está   he, she, it is/you are
esta f.   this, this one
está bem   okay
estacionar   to park
este m.   this, this one
este é?   is this?
estou   I am
estou bem   I'm well
estrangeiro m.   foreigner/abroad
estranho   strange
eu   I
exactamente   exactly
excursão f.   trip
experimentar   to try

F

fábrica f.   factory
fácil   easy
faço   I do, make
fala …?   do you, does he, she speak …?
fala bem   he, she, you speak(s) well
falo   I speak
falso   false
farmácia f.   chemist

fatia f. slice
fazer to do/make
fazer as compras to do the shopping
faz favor please
faz frio it's cold
fazes you do, make
fecha it closes
fechado closed
feio ugly
feira f. monthly market, fair
férias f. holidays
fiambre m. boiled ham
fica is situated
ficar to be situated
ficha f. form
folheto m. leaflet
fora outside, out
fraco weak
fresco fresh, chilled
fumar to smoke

G galo m. cockerel (souvenir)
garfo m. fork
garoto m. small, white coffee
garrafa f. bottle
garrafão m. demi-john
gasóleo m. diesel
gasolina f. petrol
geada f. frost
gelados m. ice-creams
gentil kind
geralmente generally
gesso m. plaster cast
ginástica f. keep-fit, P.E.
gosta de he, she, you like(s)
gostaram they, you like
gostarias you would like
gostas de visitar you like to visit
gostei I liked
gosto I like
gramas m. grammes
graus m. degrees

H há there is, there are
há quanto tempo? how much time is there?
havia there was, were
hoje today
hoje de manhã this morning

hoje em dia nowadays
hora f. hour
hora de ponta f. rush-hour
horrível awful
hotel m. hotel
houve there has been/there was

I igreja f. church
igual equal, the same
igualmente the same to you
imenso a lot, huge
inchado swollen
incluído included
indicativo m. dialling code
indigestão f. indigestion
infelizmente unfortunately
informações f. information
informática f. computers, IT
inteiro whole
internacional international
interessante interesting
inverno m. winter
ir to go
irmã f. sister
irmão brother
isto é grave this is serious

J já now, already
já escolheram? have you chosen now?
já está there you are
jantamos we dine
jantar to dine
já que given that, as
jardim m. garden
Jardim Botânico m. botanical garden
joelho m. knee
jogar to play (sport)
jornais m. newspapers
junto com together with
juntos together

L lá there
(ao) lado de next to
lago m. lake
laranja f. orange
lavabos m. toilets
lavar to wash
lembrança f. souvenir

lento slow
ler to read
levar to take, carry
linha f. platform
lindo pretty
lista f. list, menu
livraria f. bookshop
livro m. book
lixo m. rubbish
logo then, next
longe far
lugar m. place

M **mais** more
mais alguma coisa? anything else?
mais devagar more slowly
mais ou menos more or less
mala f. suitcase
mandar to send
manhã f. morning
manteiga f. butter
mas but
mau tempo m. bad weather
médico m. doctor
medida f. size
meio-dia m. midday
meia dose f. half-portion
melhor better
menos less, minus
mercado m. market
mercearia f. grocers
mês m. month
mesmo ali right over there
minutos m. minutes
morada f. address
morango m. strawberry
morno warm
mudança f. change
muitas vezes many times, often
muito very, much
muito bem very well
muito prazer pleased to meet you
museu m. museum

N **nadar** to swim
não no, not
não é? isn't it?
não, não é no, it isn't
nascimento m. birth

não seria melhor? wouldn't it be better?
nas terças on Tuesdays
natural natural
negócios m. business
nem sempre not always
nesse caso in that case
nevar to snow
neve f. snow
nome m. name
normal normal
norte m. north
nota f. note (monetary)
novo young
nublado cloudy
nuvem f. cloud

O **obrigadinho/a** thanks a lot
obrigado/a thank you
oeste m. west
olá! hi!
óleo m. oil
onde where
onde é que? where is it that?
onde fica? where is?
óptimo great
o que é que? what is it that?
ora bem well now
ora essa! come off it!
ou or
outono m. autumn
outra coisa another thing
outra vez again
ouvir to hear
ovo m. egg

P **padaria f.** baker's
país m. country
paisagem f. landscape
pão m. bread
para to, for
parque m. park
passageiro m. passenger
passar to pass, spend time
passear to stroll
pé m. foot
pechincha f. bargain
pequeno small
perguntar to ask

perigo m. danger
perto nearby
pesado heavy
péssimo awful
pessoalmente personally
pingar to drip
piscina f. swimming pool
pode he, she, you can
pois well
por by, for
porquê? why?
porque because
portanto therefore
posso? may I?
pouco little
praça f. square
practicar to practise, play (sports)
praia f. beach
prato m. plate, dish
precisa-se is needed
preencher to fill in
preferido favourite
primeiro first
procurar to look for
pronto ready
provar to taste, try
provavelmente probably

Q qual é? what, which is?
qualidade f. quality
quando when
quanto é? how much is it?
quantos? how many?
quarto m. bedroom
que? what?
queijo m. cheese
quente hot
quer? do you want?
queria I, you, he, she would like
queríamos we would like
quintal m. back yard

R rachado chipped
rápido fast
razoável reasonable
realmente really
recepção f. reception
recomendo I recommend

reformado retired
relâmpago m. lightning
relaxar to relax
remédio m. cure, medicine
reserva f. reservation
reservar to reserve
rotunda f. roundabout

S
sabe? do you know?
saber to know a fact, thing
sair to go out
sapateiro m. shoemender's
sapato m. shoe
saudável healthy
saúde f. health, cheers (drinking)
sé f. cathedral
seco dry
seguir to follow
selo m. stamp
sem without
semáforos m. traffic lights
sempre always
senhor gentleman, sir
senhora lady, madam
sentar-se to sit down
sim yes
simpático nice
só only
sobre about, over
sócio m. member
sol m. sun
solteiro single, unmarried
sou I am
subir to go up
sujo dirty

T
talho m. butcher's
também also
tanto so much
tarde f. afternoon
tem? do you have?
tempo m. weather
tinto red (wine)
típico typical
tirar to take (holidays)
torneira f. tap
trabalho m. work
trânsito m. traffic

trazer   to bring
trocar   to change, exchange
trovoada f.   thunder
tudo   everything/all

U usar   to use

V vago   vacant
vale   it's worth
vamos?   shall we go?
vários   several, various
vento m.   wind

ver   to see
verdade f.   truth
verdadeiro   true
verificar   to check
viagem f.   journey
viajar   to travel
visitar   to visit
voltar   to return
vôo m.   flight

X

xaile m.   shawl
xarope m.   medicine

Language and Topic Indexes

Numbers refer to units.